Contents

Place Value

Introduction

> I used to think place value was cheap fish 'til I learned arithmetic and spelling.

When you first learned how to do arithmetic you probably wrote your numbers with headings such as Hundreds, Tens and Units or H, T and U for short. As you became more competent you would have dropped these headings. However, it's important to remember that, even though they're invisible, those headings are still there! And there's more of them than just HTU!

1 000 000	100 000	10 000	1000	100	10	1
Millions	Hundreds of Thousands	Tens of Thousands	(units of) Thousands	Hundreds	Tens	Units
M	HTH	TTH	TH	H	T	U

Columns could go on forever.

Cheques sometimes show column headings.

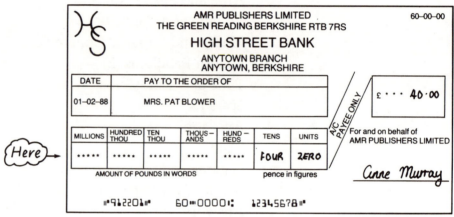

> Here →

Zero

It's really quite an important number even though it may mean nothing! If you write numbers without column headings, you need zero to make sure the other digits are under the correct but invisible column headings.

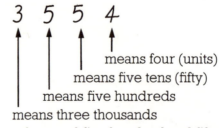

means four (units)
means five tens (fifty)
means five hundreds
means three thousands
'three thousand five hundred and fifty four'

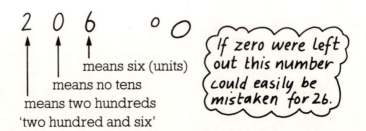

means six (units)
means no tens
means two hundreds
'two hundred and six'

> If zero were left out this number could easily be mistaken for 26.

BASIC
Arithmetic

Richard Musgrove

M
MACMILLAN
EDUCATION

Acknowledgements

The author and publishers wish to thank the following who have kindly given permission for the use of copyright materials:

British Rail Educational Service
Fine Art Wall Coverings Ltd
Grunwick Processing Laboratories Ltd
National Express Ltd
National Westminster Bank
The Post Office
Radio Times
Sealink UK Ltd
Vauxhall Motors Ltd

The publishers have made every effort to trace the copyright holders, but if they have inadvertently overlooked any, they will be pleased to make the necessary arrangements at the first opportunity.

First published 1988

Published by
MACMILLAN EDUCATION LTD
Houndmills, Basingstoke, Hampshire RG21 2XS
and London
Companies and representatives
throughout the world

Designed, typeset and illustrated by
The Pen and Ink Book Co Ltd

Produced by AMR for
Macmillan Education Ltd

Printed in Hong Kong

British Library Cataloguing in Publication Data
Musgrove, Richard
Basic Arithmetic
1. Arithmetic —— 1961 –
I. Title
513   QA107
ISBN 0 – 333 – 45136 – 8

Practice 1

Give the meaning of these figures:
a) the figure 1 in the number 2122
b) the figure 9 in the number 359
c) the figure 8 in the number 28 773
d) the figure 6 in the number 607 565

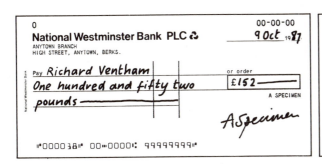 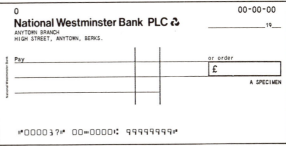

Amounts of money have to be written on cheques in both words and figures as shown above:

Practice 2

Make copies of the blank cheque and complete them for the following amounts:
a) six hundred pounds
b) seven thousand four hundred and sixty-three pounds
c) seven thousand nine hundred and nine pounds
d) £46 677
e) £82 006
f) £146 614

Practice 3

Imagine the Bank of England issued notes of £1, £10 and £100 only. How many different ways could you be given the following amounts? In each case list how it can be done.

a) £15   d) £107
b) £26   e) £111
c) £56

Which number is bigger?

You can tell which of two numbers is bigger by comparing digits with the same column headings starting from the largest values.

Example:

■ Compare 9276 and 9416:

Tʜ	H	T	U
9	2	7	6
9	4	1	6

↑ Look at this column first, both nine thousands.
Look at the hundreds next, four is bigger than two!

9416 is bigger than 9276.

■ Compare 10 042 and 998:

Tᴛʜ	Tʜ	H	T	U
1	0	0	4	2
()	()	9	9	8

↑ Look at this column first. The top number has one ten thousand and the bottom number has no ten thousands.

10 042 is bigger than 998.

Decimal numbers

Numbers less than one (unit) are also written using, often invisible, column headings:

H	T	U	.	$\frac{1}{10}$	$\frac{1}{100}$	$\frac{1}{1000}$
			decimal point	tenths t	hundredths h	thousandths th

If you write a decimal number without column headings, you need the decimal point to show where the units column belongs. The point is placed between the units and the tenths.

Reading the numbers in words

Numbers after the decimal point are read one at a time, so:

0.347 is read 'point three four seven' or 'zero point three four seven'. (The zero signifies there are no units.)
26.09 is read 'twenty six point zero nine'.
208.452 is read 'two hundred and eight point four five two'.

NB Money is an exception to this, as we will see later.

Practice 4

1 Write out the following numbers in words:
   a) 7.885
   b) 0.77
   c) 63.80
2 What is the value of zero in these numbers?
   a) 5.077
   b) 0.77
   c) 62.340
3 What is the value of the digit in brackets in the following numbers?
   a) (5) in 667.057
   b) (3) in 0.303

Size of numbers

To find out which of a pair of numbers is the bigger you compare digits starting with the ones of largest value.

Example:

■ Compare 0.72 and 0.639:

```
.t  h  th
.7  2
.6  3  9
    ↑Look at this column first.
```
0.72 is the bigger because
7 tenths is bigger than 6 tenths.

■ Compare 0.00823 and 0.006
```
0.00823
0.006
        ↑Look at this
```
column first. 0.00823 is the bigger.

Practice 5

For each group of numbers pick out the biggest:
a) 7.84   7.92
b) 6.723   6.7144
c) 2.6   6.2007
d) 29.557   29.561
e) 5.70   5.713   5.6999
f) 0.076   0.0758   0.000758
g) 0.333   0.7   0.0092   0.70

Money

It is the custom to read the pence amount after the decimal point as an ordinary number. Also, when you make out a cheque you write only the amount of pounds in words, the pence are written in figures.

■ **Example:**

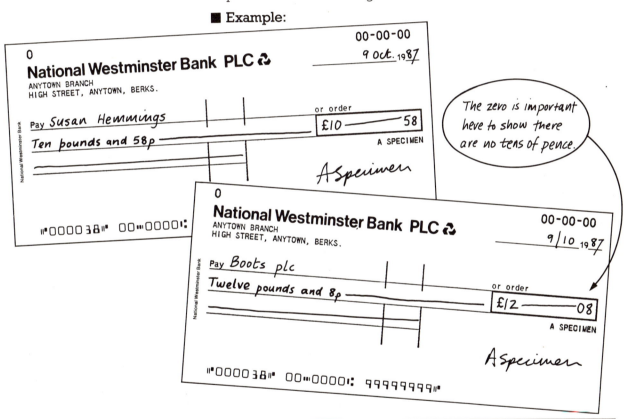

The zero is important here to show there are no tens of pence.

Practice 6

Make out cheques for the following amounts:
a) twenty-seven pounds and sixty pence
b) eight pounds and six pence
c) £342.27
d) £88.07

Commas

You often see commas used in large numbers. These are put in to split the number up and make it easier to read. A comma is put in after every third digit counting from the decimal point. This practice is becoming a bit old fashioned. Instead large numbers are written with extra wide spacing after every third digit.

Practice 7

VENTHAMS POOLS   BRISTOL

ANOTHER
ALL TIME
RECORD

MRS. SHARON SILKWOOD OF LEICESTER

£920,477

23 PTS (MAX)...£750,000.00	4 DRAWS....£424.80
22½ PTS............£ 25,246.32	
22 PTS............£ 5,192.00	12 HOMES....£ 9.36
21½ PTS............£ 1,272.14	
21 PTS............£ 209.68	6 AWAYS....£ 8.05
20½ PTS............£ 41.24	

DON'T FORGET TO SEND IN YOUR COUPON!

1 Look at the Venthams Pools payout
   Write a cheque for Mrs Sharon Silkwood's win!
   How much would you win if you had 23 points on your coupon?
   How else can you say this amount, apart from a lot!?
   Imagine you received a cheque for the 6 aways dividend.
   How would it look?
2 Non-fiction library books are put into order according to their classification code number. This is often a decimal number. Arrange these classification numbers in order, smallest first:
   628.445   627   624.176   624.25   625.7   624.1771

Practice 8

1 In the number 25 608, the value of the figure six is:
   a) six thousand   b) sixty   c) six hundred
   d) six million
   e) Put in your own answer if you do not think that a, b, c or d is correct!
2 In the number 43 216 the value of the figure two is:
   a) two tenths   b) two hundredths   c) two hundreds
   d) twenty   e) _____
3 One thousandth in figures is:
   a) 1000   b) 0.001   c) 0.01   d) 0.1000   e) _____
4 The value of the five in the number 2 588 962 is:
   a) 500 000   b) 500   c) 50   d) 5000   e) _____
5 The value of the figure five in the number 2.650 is:
   a) fifty   b) five units   c) five tenths
   d) five hundredths   e) _____
6 The number three hundred and twenty-five thousand in figures is:
   a) 325   b) 325 000   c) 3250   d) 3 250 000   e _____
7 The number two million and ten thousand in figures is:
   a) 210 000   b) 2 010 000   c) 2010   d) 2 000 010
   e) _____
8 The number 750 087 written in words is:
   a) seventy-five thousand and eighty-seven
   b) seven million fifty thousand and eighty-seven
   c) seven hundred and fifty thousand and eighty-seven
   d) seventy-five hundred and eighty-seven
   e) _____
9 The smallest of these numbers is:
   a) 0.5   b) 0.50   c) 0.050   d) 0.029   e) _____
10 The largest of these numbers is:
   a) 1 078 989   b) 999 999   c) 1 100 000
   d) 1 009 000

Whole Numbers

Introduction

You still need to be able to do calculations in your head or using pen and paper, even though electronic calculators are widely available. It would be obvious and embarrassing to check your change in a shop using a calculator, wouldn't it? If you know your multiplication tables, most simple calculations can be done much quicker in your head than with a calculator.

Before you start on a calculation, make a quick estimate in your head. What sort of size should the answer be? This is important even when you are using a calculator as you can easily get wrong answers from them if you press the wrong key by mistake!

When writing numbers keep them in the correct columns even though you probably won't be using column headings. Keep your working neat and think about what the numbers mean.

After you have completed each exercise check your answers using a calculator. If your answers disagree, check with the answers in the back. You could have made a calculator error!

Addition

Examples:

■ Add 735, 8 and 47:

Answer should be about 800.

```
  H  T  U
  7  3  5
        8
+    4  7
    2
─────────
  7  9  0
```
Answer = 790

Seems OK.

■ A car has just had an oil change at 46 785 miles. It will need one again in six thousand miles. When is the next change due?

Calculation needed is 46 785 + 6000:

Answer should be about 50 000.

```
  46785
+  6000
───────
  52785
```
Answer = 52 785 miles

Seems OK.

Practice 1

a) 467 + 264   b) 1755 + 907   c) 4007 + 809
d) 8 + 129 + 53   e) 999 + 9999   f) 24 + 204 + 2004
g) 597 + 5 + 1249   h) 7 + 525 + 8 + 296   i) 9999 + 999 + 99 + 9
j) 98 + 723 + 179

Subtraction

Examples:

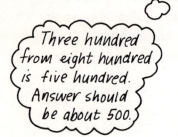

Three hundred from eight hundred is five hundred. Answer should be about 500.

■ Subtract 345 from 829:
There are two ways of doing this. Choose what you're used to.

```
H  T  U
8  2  9          ⁷8̷29              ⁴8̷29
-3 4  5          - 345      or     -⁴3̷45
                 ─────              ─────
                  484                484
```

Which are you used to?   Answer = 484

Seems OK.

■ It's 37°C in Riyadh and 18°C in London.
How much hotter is it in Riyadh?
Calculation needed is 37 − 18:

```
 37
-18
───
 19     Answer = 19°C
```

Practice 2

a) 467 − 264   b) 1755 − 907   c) 254 − 138
d) 648 − 375   e) 933 − 267   f) 903 − 194
g) 500 − 437   h) 1000 − 67   i) 2300 − 648
j) 2006 − 198

Multiplication

If you don't know your tables see the end of this chapter for some tips.

Examples:

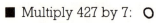

Four hundred multiplied by seven is roughly 28 hundred or 2800.

■ Multiply 427 by 7:

```
H  T  U
4  2  7
×     7
──────────
29 8  9     Answer = 2989    Seems OK.
```

■ A package holiday costs £265. What will be the total cost for four people?

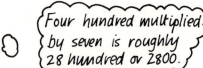

Answer should be about 3 hundred times 4; that is, 12 hundred.

Calculation needed is 265 × 4:

```
 265
×  4        Answer = 1060    Seems Ok.
────
1060
```

a) 467×2 b) 194×5 c) 254×7
d) 648×8 e) 608×9 f) 55×9
g) 2416×4 h) 3400×7 i) 3092×6
j) $142\,857 \times 6$

What happens when you multiply 142 857 by other numbers?
Investigate.

Division

There are a number of ways of writing down a division
calculation. 1623 divided by 3 can be written $1623 \div 3$ but
that doesn't help with the calculation. Usually it's worked
out like this:

3 × 5 hundred is 1500, so answer should be about 500.

3s into 1 won't go. So 3s into 16.

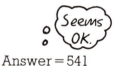

Seems OK.

$$\frac{0}{3)\overline{1623}} \qquad \frac{05}{3)\overline{11623}}$$

Th	H	T	U
	0	5	4	1

$$3)\overline{1\ {}^16\ {}^12\ 3} \qquad \text{Answer} = 541$$

The same thing could have been written $\dfrac{1623}{3}$ which is like
a fraction. (In fact, it·is a fraction!)

More examples:

■ Divide 2718 by 9:

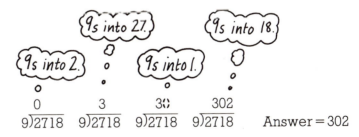

9s into 2.   *9s into 27.*   *9s into 1.*   *9s into 18.*

$$\frac{0}{9)\overline{2718}} \qquad \frac{3}{9)\overline{2718}} \qquad \frac{3\text{(}}{9)\overline{2718}} \qquad \frac{302}{9)\overline{2718}} \qquad \text{Answer} = 302$$

■ A car uses 7 gallons of petrol on a journey of 252 miles.
What is its fuel consumption in miles per gallon?

$$\begin{array}{l} \text{miles} \to 252 \\ \text{per} \to \text{—} \\ \text{gallons} \to 7 \end{array} \qquad \frac{03\ 6}{7)\overline{25^42}} \qquad \text{Answer} = 36\,\text{mpg}$$

a) $148 \div 2$ b) $711 \div 3$ c) $630 \div 3$ d) $630 \div 5$
e) $2375 \div 5$ f) $2464 \div 8$ g) $16\,200 \div 9$

h) $\dfrac{2601}{9}$ i) $\dfrac{2430}{6}$ j) $\dfrac{49\,021}{7}$

More multiplication and division

Multiplication and division by 10, 100, 1000 and so on can be done very easily, even in your head. The figures stay the same, they just move columns.

Examples:

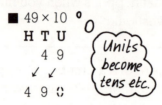

- 49 × 10

H	T	U
	4	9
	↙	↙
4	9	0

Units become tens etc.

Answer = 490

- 629 × 100

TTh	Th	H	T	U
		6	2	9
	↙	↙	↙	
6	2	9	0	0

Units become hundreds.

Answer = 62 900

- 1620 ÷ 10

Th	H	T	U
1	6	2	0
	↘	↘	↘
	1	6	2

Answer = 162

- 32 × 200

Th	H	T	U
		3	2
	↙	↙	
3	2	0	0
↓	↓	↓	↓
6	4	0	0

Answer = 6400

Practice 5

a) 26 × 10
b) 17 × 100
c) 460 ÷ 10
d) 189 × 100
e) 7000 ÷ 100
f) 86 000 ÷ 10
g) 60 000 ÷ 1000
h) 276 × 100
i) 99 × 1000
j) 24 × 200

Long multiplication

This is the name given to multiplication by numbers bigger than 10. It is set out like this example:

Example:

- 628 × 32

Two ways again!

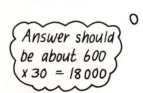

Answer should be about 600 × 30 = 18 000

```
    628
 ×   32
  1 256   ← that's 628 × 2
 18 840   ← that's 628 × 30
 20 096
```

```
    628
 ×   32
 18 840   ← that's 628 × 30
  1 256   ← that's 628 × 2
 20 096
```

More examples:

- 367×35 is the same as 35×367

$$367 \times 35$$

367	
$\times$ 35	
1835	$\leftarrow 367 \times 5$
11 010	$\leftarrow 367 \times 30$
12 845	

35	
$\times$ 367	
245	$\leftarrow 35 \times 7$
2 100	$\leftarrow 35 \times 60$
10 500	$\leftarrow 35 \times 300$
12 845	

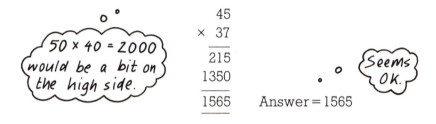

You get the same answer whichever way you do it.

- A hall has been set out with chairs. There are 45 rows each with 37 chairs. How many people will the hall seat? Calculation needed 45×37:

50 × 40 = 2000 would be a bit on the high side.

45	
$\times$ 37	
215	
1350	
1565	Answer = 1565

Seems OK.

Practice 6

a) 148×24 b) 194×52 c) 263×148

d) 332×50 e) 46×600 f) 32×4344

g) $16 \times 52\,408$ h) $142\,857 \times 16$ i) 111×111

j) 1111×1111

Investigate the pattern which builds up.

Remainders

Quite often a division sum does not work out exactly.

Example:

■ Divide 345 by 9:

$$9\overline{)3\,^{3}4\,^{7}5}\,^{→3}$$
$$\quad 0\ 3\ 8$$

9s into 75?
9 × 8 = 72 so it's
8 nines with 3
left over.

The value left over, in this case 3, is called the *remainder*. Dealing with the remainder takes us into fractions and decimals. Sometimes it is enough to know what the remainder is.

Practice 7

What is the remainder when you divide the following?
a) you divide 123 by 7, by 9, by 2, by 3
b) you divide 1000 by 7, by 11, by 100, by 33
c) you divide 1001 by 3, by 5, by 7, by 11, by 13

Practice 8

Write down the calculation involved in each of these situations. You don't have to do it! Yet!

a) At the beginning of a quarter a gas meter reads 37 649, at the end it reads 48 002. How much gas has been used during the quarter?
b) 55 boxes each contain half a dozen eggs. How many eggs are there in all?
c) 1000 people are expected at a meeting in a hall. Chairs have to be set out in rows of 25. How many rows are required?
d) A person is offered £1000 part exchange on a secondhand car costing £3450. How much more money does this person need to find?
e) A £4500 prize on a spot-the-ball competition is shared by three people. How much do they each get?
f) What's the difference in price between a new Mini Metro (£4671) and a new Citroen Visa (£3933)?

g) What is the distance between Bettyhill and John o'Groats?

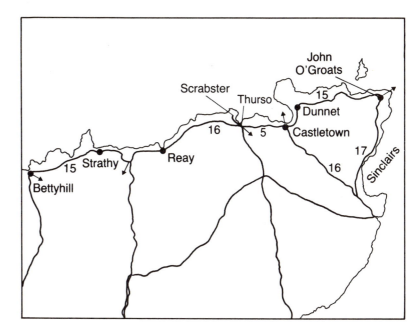

h) A car does 35 miles to the gallon. Its tank holds 12 gallons. What is the car's range?

Now do each of the calculations.

Multiplication tables

You should learn your multiplication tables from 2 × 2 up to 9 × 9. This involves a total of only 36 combinations. Work it out remembering that 7 × 8 is the same as 8 × 7. To test yourself and to improve your speed, try filling in the table below against the clock. You can repeat this exercise by drawing up a similar table but change the order of the numbers each time.

X	4	7	10	2	9	8	5	3	6
6									
3			30						
5									
8									
9									
2						*			
10									
7									
4									

In this square you'd put 2 × 8 = 16

Decimals

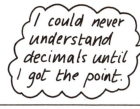

Introduction

Decimal numbers have become much more important than they used to be. This is largely because of the change to the metric system of measurement. For instance, weight is now often measured in kilograms instead of pounds. The metric system is easy to use if you understand and can work with decimals.

Addition

This should cause you no problems provided you keep the numbers in columns. The decimal point helps you do this. Simply write the numbers with the decimal points in a vertical line above each other.

Examples:

■ $12.67 + 7.4$

$$
\begin{array}{r}
12.67 \\
+\ 7.40 \leftarrow \\
\hline
20.07
\end{array}
$$

A zero belongs here but generally it's not written.

■ $6.9 + 12 + 0.098 + 3.45$

$$
\begin{array}{r}
6.9 \\
12 \leftarrow \\
0.098 \\
3.45 \\
\hline
22.448
\end{array}
$$

You could put lots of zeros in the gaps.

Practice 1

a) $2.34 + 4.67$ b) $4.9 + 7.63$ c) $0.63 + 8.7$
d) $23.6 + 7.4$ e) $0.94 + 0.072$ f) $12 + 8.45$
g) $4.6 + 13.8 + 7.9$ h) $5.3 + 6 + 12.87$ i) $12.7 + 60 + 0.35 + 7$
j) $0.009 + 0.064$

Subtraction

As in addition, keep the numbers with the decimal points above each other. Sometimes you will need to put in one or more zeros in the sum, but you must never change the value of either of the numbers.

Examples:

■ $12.67 - 2.4$

$$
\begin{array}{r}
12.67 \\
-\ 2.40 \\
\hline
10.27
\end{array}
$$

■ $9 - 4.6$

$$
\begin{array}{r}
9.0 \leftarrow \\
-\ 4.6 \\
\hline
4.4
\end{array}
$$

You need a zero here.

■ $100 - 7.8$

$$
\begin{array}{r}
100.0 \\
-\ 7.8 \\
\hline
92.2
\end{array}
$$

Practice 2

a) $4.67 - 2.64$ b) $7.63 - 4.87$ c) $23.62 - 5.94$
d) $46.70 - 2.64$ e) $46.7 - 8.88$ f) $0.73 - 0.263$
g) $10 - 2.7$ h) $10 - 0.74$ i) $1 - 0.455$
j) $6 - 0.072$

Multiplication

Examples:

■ 5.44 × 3

$$\begin{array}{r} 5.44 \\ \times \quad 3 \\ \hline 16.32 \end{array}$$

■ 5.44 × 1000

Th H T U.th
5.44

5 4 4 0. Answer = 5440.

Practice 3

a) 7.62 × 2   b) 26.4 × 6   c) 24.2 × 5
d) 0.0763 × 8   e) 0.834 × 7   f) 7.62 × 10
g) 0.0073 × 10   h) 5.6 × 1000   i) 0.082 × 100
j) 32.67 × 100

Division

Examples:

■ 26.34 ÷ 2

$$\begin{array}{r} 13.17 \\ 2\overline{)26.34} \end{array}$$

Answer = 13.17

■ 75.15 ÷ 5

$$\begin{array}{r} 1\ 5.03 \\ 5\overline{)7^25.1^15} \end{array}$$

Answer = 15.03

■ 5.1 ÷ 8

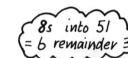

$$\begin{array}{r} 0\ 6\ 3\ 7\ 5 \\ 8\overline{)5.5^13^06^04^00} \end{array}$$

Answer = 0.6375

Practice 4

a) 31.6 ÷ 2   b) 7.11 ÷ 9   c) 0.2032 ÷ 2
d) 7.227 ÷ 3   e) 0.2124 ÷ 3   f) 6.1272 ÷ 9
g) 7.1 ÷ 2   h) 0.621 ÷ 4   i) 0.7 ÷ 8
j) 31 ÷ 8   k) 1.2 ÷ 9   l) 5 ÷ 7
m) 4.72 ÷ 10   n) 0.24 ÷ 1000   o) 3.73 ÷ 100

More multiplication

Examples:

■ 2.6 × 0.8

Treat this as 26 × 8 and put the decimal point in afterwards.

$$\begin{array}{r} 26 \\ \times \quad 8 \\ \hline 208 \\ \hline 4 \end{array}$$

26← This is ten times bigger than 2.6
× 8← This is ten times bigger than 0.8

So this answer is a hundred (10 × 10) bigger than required.

Therefore, 2.6 × 0.8 = 2.08

Alternatively:

2.6   ×   0.8   =   2.08
■   ■   ■
↑   ↑   ↑
one place   one place   two places
of decimals of decimals of decimals

This gives us a quick and easy way of working out where the decimal point goes in the answer.

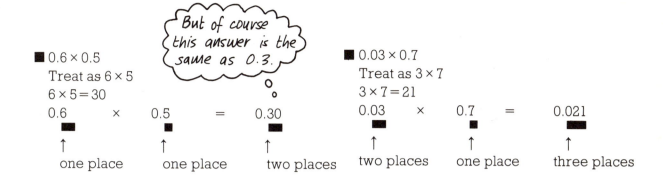

■ 0.6×0.5

Treat as 6×5

$6 \times 5 = 30$

$$0.6 \quad \times \quad 0.5 \quad = \quad 0.30$$

↑ one place ↑ one place ↑ two places

But of course this answer is the same as 0.3.

■ 0.03×0.7

Treat as 3×7

$3 \times 7 = 21$

$$0.03 \quad \times \quad 0.7 \quad = \quad 0.021$$

↑ two places ↑ one place ↑ three places

Practice 5

a) 2.5×0.3 b) 0.7×0.6 c) 0.6×0.03

d) 1.6×1.2 e) 0.04×0.5 f) 0.2×1.4

g) 16×0.4 h) 0.6×25 i) 0.02×0.06

j) 2.3×3.1

More division

Examples:

What do you have to multiply by to make divisor, 0.2, a whole number?
$0.2 \times 10 = 2$

■ $0.5 \div 0.2$

$$0.5 \div 0.2 = \frac{0.5}{0.2} = \frac{0.5 \times 10}{0.2 \times 10} = \frac{5}{2} = 2\overline{)5.0}^{\,2.5}$$

$0.5 \div 0.2 = 2.5$

What do you multiply by to make 0.03 a whole number?
$0.03 \times 10 = 0.3$, no good, but $0.03 \times 100 = 3$, fine!

■ $1.2 \div 0.03 = \frac{1.2}{0.03} = \frac{1.2 \times 100}{0.03 \times 100} = \frac{120}{3} = 3\overline{)120}^{\,40}$

$1.2 \div 0.03 = 40$

Practice 6

a) $0.4 \div 0.5$ b) $2.1 \div 0.7$ c) $0.75 \div 0.3$

d) $10 \div 0.4$ e) $0.8 \div 0.04$ f) $1 \div 0.05$

g) $1.6 \div 0.08$ h) $100 \div 0.2$ i) $25 \div 0.4$

j) $1 \div 0.25$

New sums from old

If you know the answer to one sum, it can sometimes be an easy step to the answer of a similar sum.

We know $^{142.4}/_4$, so split 400 into 4×100.

We know $^{142.4}/_4 = 35.6$ so $142.4 = 35.6 \times 4$.

Example:

■ Given that $142.4 \div 4 = 35.6$, what is the answer to these?

a) $142.4 \div 400$ b) 35.6×40

a) $142.4 \div 400$ is $\dfrac{142.4}{400} = \dfrac{142.4 \times \frac{1}{100}}{4} = 35.6 \times \dfrac{1}{100} = 0.356$

b) 35.6×40 is $35.6 \times 4 \times 10 = 142.4 \times 10 = 1424.0$

Practice 7

Given that:
a) $22.2 \times .7 = 15.54$
b) $62.1 \div 9 = 6.9$
c) $7.11 \div 30 = 0.237$
d) $16.8 \times 0.95 = 15.96$
e) $0.66 \times 95 = 6.27$
f) $8.2 \times 7.3 = 59.86$
g) $1298 \div 55 = 23.6$
h) $1053 \div 450 = 2.34$

What is the answer to these?
$15.54 \div 22.2$
$62.1 \div 90$
2.37×300
$15.96 \div 0.95$
$6.27 \div 0.95$
$598.6 \div 73$
$129.8 \div 5.5$
234×0.45

Money

Situations involving money are the most common examples of decimal calculations being used in everyday life. With money the decimal number is restricted to two decimal places because you can't have an amount less than a penny which is one hundredth of a pound (£0.01).

Practice 8

In each situation first write down the calculation involved before you work it out. Most of these involve money.

a) Three people eat a meal in a restaurant. The bill totals £13.41, which they split equally amongst them. How much does each pay?
b) How much do seven 18p stamps cost?
c) At the beginning of a short journey a car's mileage shows 26 735.6, at the end 26 762.1. What was the journey distance?
d) A bag of sugar weighs 2.2 kg. How much do eight bags weigh?
e) Four items from a Chinese takeaway cost £1.65, £1.75, £2.25 and 65p. What is the total cost?
f) A supermarket bill is £7.83. How much change would you get from a £20 note?
g) What is the cost of a gallon of petrol (4.5 litres) at 33.1p per litre?
h) Normal body temperature is 98.4°F. A sick person has a temperature of 100.2°F. How much is this above normal?

Powers, Roots, Factors and Multiples

Powers

'Four to the power three' means $\underbrace{4 \times 4 \times 4}$ and is written 4^3.

Three lots of four are multiplied together.

The value of 4^3 is $\underbrace{4 \times 4} \times 4 = 64$

16×4

5^2 means 5×5 and so $5^2 = 25$

'Five to the power two' is often called '5 squared'.

'Four to the power three' is called '4 cubed'.

Practice 1

Can you give the value of these?

a) 9^2 b) 3^4 c) 2^4

d) 13^2 e) 2^6 f) $(0.7)^2$

g) $(0.2)^2$ h) $(0.5)^2$ i) $(1.2)^2$

j) $(1.1)^2$

Brackets

Whenever you see brackets in a mathematical expression you should calculate what's inside the brackets before you do anything else!

Example: ∘ O *See the difference the brackets make.*

■ $(7 + 2)^2 \rightarrow 7 + 2 = 9 \rightarrow (7 + 2)^2 = 9^2 = 81$

If there are no brackets you work out the powers before $\div$, $\times$, $+$ or $-$.

Examples:

■ $7 + 2^2 \rightarrow 2^2 = 4 \rightarrow 7 + 2^2 = 7 + 4 = 11$

■ $5^2 - 2^2 \rightarrow 5^2 = 25 \rightarrow 2^2 = 4 \rightarrow 5^2 - 2^2 = 25 - 4 = 21$

Practice 2

a) $6^2 - 3^2$ b) 5×4^2 c) $3^2 + 4^2 - 5^2$

d) $\frac{1}{4}$ of 10^2 e) $(2 \times 3)^2$ f) $2^3 \times 4$

g) 1.9×10^2 h) $4^3 - 2^3$ i) $6^2 - 5^2 + 2^2$

j) $7^2 - 3^3$ k) $(0.8 + 0.2)^2$ l) $(1.7 - 0.8)^2$

m) $(8 \times 0.25)^2$ n) $(5 \div 2)^2$ o) $6 \div 10^2$

Powers of ten

Powers of ten make a simple pattern and so they are easy to work out. Numbers written like 6×10^3 are very common.

$$10^1 = 10$$
$$10^2 = 10 \times 10 = 100$$
$$10^3 = 10 \times 10 \times 10 = 1000$$
$$10^4 = 10 \times 10 \times 10 \times 10 = 10\,000$$

Square roots

5 squared is $5^2 = 5 \times 5 = 25$

We also call 5 the square root of 25 and this is written $\sqrt{25}$.

That is, $\sqrt{25} = $ 5 because $5 \times 5 = 25$
$\sqrt{49} = $ 7 because $7 \times 7 = 49$
$\sqrt{400} = 20$ because $20 \times 20 = 400$

Practice 3

What are the square roots of these numbers?

a) $\sqrt{64}$ b) $\sqrt{100}$ c) $\sqrt{81}$

d) $\sqrt{144}$ e) $\sqrt{169}$ f) $\sqrt{625}$

g) $\sqrt{441}$ h) $\sqrt{121}$ i) $\sqrt{676}$

j) $\sqrt{900}$

Multiples

The multiples of 8 are the numbers given by the eight times table:

$1 \times 8 = $ 8
$2 \times 8 = $ 16
$3 \times 8 = $ 24
$4 \times 8 = $ 32   These are the multiples of eight.
$5 \times 8 = $ 40   ←
$6 \times 8 = $ 48
$7 \times 8 = $ 56
$8 \times 8 = $ 64

The multiples of eight are 8, 16, 24, 32, 40, 48, 56, and so on. You don't stop at 80 or 96.
The multiples of any other number are found in the same way.

Examples:

■ What are the multiples of seven between 30 and 50?
Count in sevens (the 7 × table):

7 . . . 14 . . . 21 . . . 28 . . . 35 . . . 42 . . . 49 . . . 56 . . . 63 . . .

These are the multiples between 30 and 50: 35, 42 and 49

■ What is the smallest number into which 8 and 6 will divide exactly?

The multiples of 8 are 8 . . . 16 . . . 24 . . . 32 . . . 40 . . . 48 . . . 56 . . . 64 . . .
The multiples of 6 are 6 . . . 12 . . . 18 . . . 24 . . . 30 . . . 36 . . . 42 . . . 48 . . .
The first number to occur in *both* rows is 24.
24 is the smallest number into which both 8 and 6 will divide exactly.

Practice 4

What is the smallest number into which these numbers will divide?
a) 9 and 6 b) 4 and 9 c) 10 and 8 d) 7 and 14
e) 9 and 12

Practice 5

What are the multiples of these numbers?
a) 7 between 60 and 69?
b) 4 between 60 and 69
c) 5 between 60 and 69
d) 19 between 60 and 69
e) 13 between 60 and 69

Factors

A *factor* of a number is a number which will divide into it exactly, that is without leaving a remainder.

6 divides into 42 so 6 is a factor of 42.

$42 \div 6 = 7$ so $42 \div 7 = 6$ so 7 is also a factor of 42. Factors come in pairs.

42 has other factors as well, 1 (simple) and 42,

also 2 and 21 since $2 \times 21 = 42$
and 3 and 14 since $3 \times 14 = 42$

The factors of 42 are 1, 2, 3, 6, 7, 14, 21, 42.

Practice 6

What are the factors of these numbers?
a) 15 b) 60 c) 43 d) 36 e) 50 f) 31 g) 32 h) 90

Common factors

36 has factors 1, 2, 3, 4, 6, 9, 12, 18 and 36.
30 has factors 1, 2, 3, 5, 6, 10, 15 and 30.

1, 2, 3 and 6 are factors of both 30 and 36. They are sometimes known as *common factors*.

Example:

■ What is the biggest factor common to both 45 and 27?
45 has factors 1, 3, 5, 9, 15, 45
27 has factors 1, 3, 9, 27
So 9 is the biggest common factor.

Practice 7

What are the biggest factors common to these numbers?
a) 40 and 56
b) 35 and 49
c) 70 and 80
d) 35 and 37
e) 200 and 190

Practice 8

1 What is the value of 5^3?
   a) 15   b) 125   c) 243   d) 25   e) _____
2 Which of the following is a multiple of 8?
   a) 61   b) 60   c) 64   d) 74   e) none
3 What is the value of $6 + 3^2$?
   a) 15   b) 81   c) 45   d) 39   e) _____
4 Which of these numbers is a factor of 513?
   a) 7   b) 5   c) 9   d) 11   e) none
5 What is the square root of 729?
   a) 25   b) 26   c) 27   d) 28   e) _____
6 What is the value of 2.5×10^2?
   a) 625   b) 0.025   c) 2.500   d) 250   e) _____
7 Which of these numbers is a factor of both 819 and 119?
   a) 9   b) 13   c) 17   d) 7   e) none
8 What is the value of $(4 + 7)^2$?
   a) 65   b) 53   c) 121   d) 23   e) _____
9 What is the biggest factor common to both 42 and 66?
   a) 6   b) 14   c) 33   d) 2   e) _____
10 What is the smallest number into which 14 and 6 will divide?
   a) 28   b) 21   c) 84   d) 42   e) _____

Fractions – Basic Ideas

A *fraction* is part of a whole.

If the 'whole' is represented by the circle below, then the fraction 'three quarters' is represented by the parts of the circle which are shaded:

This fraction is written $\frac{3}{4}$.

The number at the bottom tells you how many *equal* parts the 'whole' is divided up into. The number at the top says how many parts are shaded.

The 'whole' can be any shape or object. Here's a rectangle:

You can show the same fraction in more than one way. $\frac{1}{6}$ for instance, could be this: or this:

 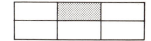

pronounced 'one sixth'.

But the parts that the 'whole' is divided up into must be *equal*.

does not show $\frac{1}{6}$

Practice 1

On each of these shapes shade the fraction given:

a)   b)   c)   d)   e)

⊕ $\frac{1}{4}$ △ $\frac{2}{3}$ ⊞ $\frac{7}{9}$ ⊞ $\frac{5}{12}$ ⊞ $\frac{1}{4}$

One eighth ($\frac{1}{8}$) can be thought as 'a whole divided by eight', $1 \div 8$.

In the same way $\frac{3}{8}$ could be thought as 'three wholes divided by eight', $3 \div 8$.

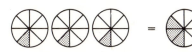

$\frac{3}{8}$ is another way of writing $3 \div 8$.

Equivalent fractions

Consider how this rectangle has been shaded:

You could say it was $\frac{1}{3}$ or $\frac{4}{12}$, both fractions are correct. We say $\frac{1}{3}$ is *equivalent* to $\frac{4}{12}$.

Here are some other examples of equivalent fractions:

 $\frac{2}{8} = \frac{1}{4}$ $\frac{2}{5} = \frac{8}{20}$ $\frac{3}{4} = \frac{12}{16}$

Practice 2

Write down the fraction shaded in two different ways:

a)   b)   c)   d)   e)

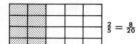
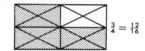

You can work out equivalent fractions without drawing shapes and shading them. The quickest way is like this:

$$\frac{5}{7} = \frac{10}{14} = \frac{15}{21} = \quad \begin{array}{l}\leftarrow\text{top row : multiples of 5}\\ \leftarrow\text{bottom row : multiples of 7}\end{array}$$

Practice 3

Write out the first ten fractions equivalent to these fractions.

a) $\frac{4}{5}$ d) $\frac{1}{7}$

b) $\frac{2}{3}$ e) $\frac{7}{10}$

c) $\frac{6}{11}$

Provided you multiply the top and bottom of a fraction by the same number you will get an equivalent fraction:

$$\frac{5}{7} \xrightarrow[\times 6]{\times 6} \frac{30}{42}$$

Example:

■ $\frac{2}{5}$ is equivalent to how many thirtieths?

$$\frac{2}{5} = \frac{?}{30} \qquad \frac{2}{5} \xrightarrow[\times 6]{} \frac{?}{30} \qquad \frac{2}{5} \xrightarrow[\times 6]{\times 6} \frac{12}{30}.$$

Practice 4

Copy and complete the following fractions:

a) $\frac{3}{4} = \frac{?}{16}$ d) $\frac{2}{5} = \frac{14}{?}$

b) $\frac{2}{7} = \frac{?}{21}$ e) $\frac{7}{8} = \frac{14}{?}$

c) $\frac{1}{9} = \frac{?}{45}$

Simplified fractions

A fraction can sometimes be simplified into an equivalent fraction that uses smaller numbers. Provided you divide top and bottom by the same number you will always get another equivalent fraction.

$$\frac{2}{14} \xrightarrow[\div 2]{\div 2} \frac{1}{7}$$

To simplify a fraction, you ask yourself: 'Do the top number and the bottom number have a common factor?' If so, this is what you divide by. To express a fraction in its lowest terms, you repeat the process until there is no common factor for top and bottom numbers.

$$\frac{12}{18} \xrightarrow[\div 2]{\div 2} \frac{6}{9} \xrightarrow[\div 3]{\div 3} \frac{2}{3}$$

Practice 5

Express these fractions in their lowest terms:

a) $\frac{3}{9}$ c) $\frac{12}{15}$ e) $\frac{4}{63}$ g) $\frac{7}{30}$ i) $\frac{15}{20}$

b) $\frac{8}{36}$ d) $\frac{56}{77}$ f) $\frac{18}{35}$ h) $\frac{15}{36}$ j) $\frac{63}{81}$

Which is bigger?

It is sometimes easy to see which of two fractions is the bigger. For instance, $\frac{3}{4}$ is bigger than $\frac{1}{2}$.

Sometimes it is not easy to see which is bigger. Compare $\frac{5}{7}$ with $\frac{3}{4}$.

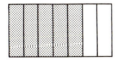 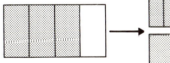 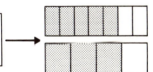

There's an easier way to tell which fraction is bigger. Rather than draw accurate diagrams you can use equivalent fractions:

$$\frac{5}{7} = \frac{10}{14} = \frac{15}{21} = \boxed{\frac{20}{28}} = \frac{25}{35} = \frac{30}{42}$$

$$\frac{3}{4} = \frac{6}{8} = \frac{9}{12} = \frac{12}{16} = \frac{15}{20} = \frac{18}{24} = \boxed{\frac{21}{28}} \qquad \frac{21}{28} \text{ is bigger than } \frac{20}{28}$$

So $\frac{3}{4}$ is bigger than $\frac{5}{7}$.

Practice 6

Which is the bigger fraction?

a) $\frac{2}{5}$ or $\frac{1}{3}$ d) $\frac{4}{9}$ or $\frac{3}{7}$ g) $\frac{3}{8}$ or $\frac{1}{3}$ j) $\frac{2}{7}$ or $\frac{5}{21}$

b) $\frac{5}{6}$ or $\frac{3}{4}$ e) $\frac{4}{7}$ or $\frac{3}{5}$ h) $\frac{9}{11}$ or $\frac{6}{7}$

c) $\frac{2}{9}$ or $\frac{3}{11}$ f) $\frac{4}{12}$ or $\frac{1}{3}$ i) $\frac{1}{5}$ or $\frac{3}{14}$

Four Rules of Fractions _____

Addition and subtraction

You can add or subtract two fractions if they have the same bottom number.

$$\frac{3}{11}+\frac{7}{11}=\frac{10}{11} \qquad \frac{6}{7}-\frac{2}{7}=\frac{4}{7}$$

If the fractions have different bottom numbers, before you can add or subtract, you have to change them into equivalent fractions *with the same bottom numbers.*

$$\frac{1}{6}+\frac{1}{4}\rightarrow\frac{1}{6}\xrightarrow[\times 2]{\times 2}\frac{2}{12} \rightarrow\frac{1}{6}+\frac{1}{4} \qquad \rightarrow\frac{1}{6}+\frac{1}{4}=\frac{5}{12}$$

$$\frac{1}{4}\xrightarrow[\times 3]{\times 3}\frac{3}{12} \qquad \frac{2}{12}+\frac{3}{12}=\frac{5}{12}$$

Practice 1

a) $\frac{3}{5}+\frac{1}{10}$ b) $\frac{1}{4}+\frac{5}{8}$ c) $\frac{2}{3}+\frac{1}{9}$ d) $\frac{1}{3}+\frac{5}{12}$ e) $\frac{3}{8}+\frac{5}{12}$

f) $\frac{2}{7}+\frac{1}{5}$ g) $\frac{2}{5}+\frac{3}{8}$ h) $\frac{4}{9}+\frac{3}{7}$ i) $\frac{1}{6}+\frac{7}{10}$ j) $\frac{3}{4}+\frac{3}{14}$

k) $\frac{3}{5}-\frac{1}{10}$ l) $\frac{5}{8}-\frac{1}{4}$ m) $\frac{2}{3}-\frac{1}{9}$ n) $\frac{7}{12}-\frac{1}{3}$ o) $\frac{11}{12}-\frac{3}{8}$

p) $\frac{6}{7}-\frac{3}{5}$ q) $\frac{4}{5}-\frac{3}{7}$ r) $\frac{8}{9}-\frac{2}{3}$ s) $\frac{7}{10}-\frac{2}{15}$ t) $\frac{3}{4}-\frac{5}{18}$

Top heavy fractions

If the top number is bigger than the bottom number in a fraction it is sometimes known as a *top heavy* fraction. A fraction which is top heavy can be changed into a whole number and fraction:

$$\frac{11}{3}\rightarrow\frac{3}{3}=1 \text{ whole} \qquad \frac{9}{3}=3 \text{ wholes}\rightarrow\frac{11}{3}=\frac{9+2}{3}\rightarrow\frac{11}{3}=3\frac{2}{3}$$

A whole number and fraction called a *mixed number* can be changed into a top heavy fraction.

$$4\frac{2}{5}\rightarrow 4 \text{ wholes}=4\times\frac{5}{5}=\frac{20}{5}\rightarrow 4\frac{2}{5}=\frac{20}{5}+\frac{2}{5}=\frac{22}{5}$$

Practice 2

Change these into whole numbers and fractions:

a) $\frac{25}{6}$ b) $\frac{17}{3}$ c) $\frac{17}{9}$ d) $\frac{25}{11}$ e) $\frac{35}{5}$

Practice 3

Change these into top heavy fractions:

a) $1\frac{5}{8}$ b) $7\frac{3}{4}$ c) $5\frac{2}{5}$ d) $3\frac{4}{9}$ e) $4\frac{1}{8}$

More addition and subtraction

Examples:

■ a) $\frac{3}{10} + \frac{7}{8}$

$$\frac{3}{10} + \frac{7}{8} \to \frac{3}{10} \xrightarrow[\times 4]{\times 4} \frac{12}{40}$$

$$\frac{7}{8} \xrightarrow[\times 5]{\times 5} \frac{35}{40}$$

$$\frac{12}{40} + \frac{35}{40} = \frac{47}{40} \to \frac{40}{40} = 1$$

$$\frac{3}{10} + \frac{7}{8} = 1\frac{7}{40}$$

■ b) $2\frac{3}{5} + 3\frac{4}{5}$

$$2\frac{3}{5} + 3\frac{4}{5} \to 2 + 3 = 5$$

$$\frac{3}{5} + \frac{4}{5} = \frac{7}{5} \to \frac{5}{5} = 1$$

$$\to \frac{7}{5} = 1\frac{2}{5}$$

$$2\frac{3}{5} + 3\frac{4}{5} = 5 + 1\frac{2}{5} = 6\frac{2}{5}$$

Practice 4

a) $\frac{5}{6} + \frac{5}{6}$ b) $\frac{2}{7} + \frac{11}{14}$ c) $\frac{2}{5} + \frac{11}{15}$ d) $\frac{1}{2} + \frac{3}{4} + \frac{7}{8}$ e) $\frac{4}{9} + \frac{5}{6}$

f) $\frac{1}{3} + \frac{5}{6} + \frac{3}{4}$ g) $\frac{7}{16} + \frac{9}{16}$ h) $\frac{7}{10} + \frac{5}{8}$ i) $1\frac{3}{5} + 1\frac{2}{5}$ j) $2\frac{1}{2} + \frac{5}{8}$

k) $1\frac{4}{9} + \frac{2}{3}$ l) $2\frac{1}{3} + \frac{3}{4}$ m) $1\frac{4}{5} + 1\frac{3}{10}$ n) $2\frac{1}{2} + 3\frac{5}{9}$ o) $2\frac{4}{9} + 5\frac{2}{3}$

Examples:

■ a) $3\frac{1}{2} - 1\frac{3}{8}$

$$3\frac{1}{2} - 1\frac{3}{8} \to 3 - 1 = 2$$

$$\to 2\frac{1}{2} - \frac{3}{8} = 2\frac{4}{8} - \frac{3}{8} = 2\frac{1}{8}$$

$$3\frac{1}{2} - 1\frac{3}{8} = 2\frac{1}{8}$$

■ b) $4\frac{3}{8} - 1\frac{1}{2}$

$$4\frac{3}{8} - 1\frac{1}{2} \to 4 - 1 = 3$$

$$3\frac{3}{8} - \frac{1}{2} = 3\frac{3}{8} - \frac{4}{8}$$

Can't do without changing the whole number.

$$\to 3 = 2\frac{8}{8}$$

$$\to 3\frac{3}{8} = 2\frac{11}{8} \to 2\frac{11}{8} - \frac{4}{8} = 2\frac{7}{8}$$

Practice 5

a) $1\frac{5}{6} - \frac{8}{9}$ b) $3\frac{3}{4} - 1\frac{13}{14}$ c) $1\frac{7}{16} - \frac{1}{4}$ d) $1\frac{3}{8} - \frac{3}{4}$ e) $4\frac{2}{5} - 1\frac{7}{10}$

f) $1 - \frac{11}{16}$ g) $4 - \frac{8}{9}$ h) $3 - 1\frac{2}{3}$ i) $5 - \frac{11}{15}$ j) $2\frac{1}{2} - 1\frac{11}{17}$

Multiplication

Examples:

■ a) $\frac{2}{7} \times \frac{3}{11}$

$$\to 2 \times 3 = 6$$

$$\to 7 \times 11 = 77$$

$$\to \frac{2}{7} \times \frac{3}{11} = \frac{6}{77}$$

■ b) $\frac{4}{5}$ of $\frac{7}{8}$

$$\frac{4}{5} \text{ of } \frac{7}{8} = \frac{4}{5} \times \frac{7}{8} = \frac{28}{40}$$

$$\to \frac{28}{40} \xrightarrow[\div 4]{\div 4} \frac{7}{10}$$

$$\to \frac{4}{5} \text{ of } \frac{7}{8} = \frac{7}{10}$$

Practice 6

a) $\frac{2}{3} \times \frac{5}{9}$ b) $\frac{5}{16} \times \frac{4}{9}$ c) $\frac{3}{20} \times \frac{4}{21}$ d) $\frac{5}{21} \times \frac{14}{15}$ e) $\frac{10}{9} \times \frac{3}{25}$

f) $\frac{1}{3}$ of $\frac{3}{4}$ g) $\frac{1}{5}$ of $\frac{10}{11}$ h) $\frac{1}{9}$ of $\frac{6}{7}$ i) $\frac{2}{5}$ of $\frac{1}{6}$ j) $\frac{3}{4}$ of $\frac{10}{21}$

Example:

■ $\frac{2}{3}$ of 36 $\qquad$ $\frac{2}{3}$ of $36 = \frac{2}{3} \times 36$

$\rightarrow$ 36 as a fraction is $\frac{36}{1} \rightarrow \frac{2}{3} \times \frac{36}{1} = \frac{72}{3} \xrightarrow[\div 3]{\div 3} \frac{24}{1} = 24$

Practice 7

a) $\frac{1}{2} \times 60$　b) $\frac{1}{5} \times 35$　　c) $12 \times \frac{5}{6}$　d) $20 \times \frac{5}{8}$　e) $\frac{1}{4}$ of 30

f) $\frac{3}{5}$ of 25　g) 4 lots of $\frac{5}{8}$　h) $\frac{2}{9}$ of 33　i) $\frac{7}{10} \times 9$　j) $\frac{7}{8} \times 18$

Examples:

■ a) $3\frac{1}{2} \times \frac{10}{21}$ ○ ○ *This change to a top heavy fraction **must** be made.*

$\rightarrow 3\frac{1}{2} = \frac{7}{2}$

$\rightarrow 3\frac{1}{2} \times \frac{10}{21} = \frac{7}{2} \times \frac{10}{21} = \frac{70}{42}$

$\frac{70}{42} = \frac{10}{6} = \frac{5}{3}$

■ b) $2\frac{1}{4} \times 1\frac{1}{3}$ ○ ○ *Both numbers **must** be changed into fractions.*

$\rightarrow 2\frac{1}{4} = \frac{9}{4} \rightarrow 1\frac{1}{3} = \frac{4}{3}$

$\rightarrow 2\frac{1}{4} \times 1\frac{1}{3} = \frac{9}{4} \times \frac{4}{3} = \frac{36}{12} = 3$

Practice 8

a) $2\frac{1}{2} \times \frac{7}{10}$　b) $3\frac{2}{3} \times \frac{1}{11}$　c) $4\frac{2}{7} \times 1\frac{1}{6}$　d) $3\frac{1}{5} \times 1\frac{3}{4}$　e) $1\frac{3}{7} \times \frac{7}{3}$

f) $2\frac{2}{9} \times 5\frac{1}{4}$　g) $1\frac{1}{5} \times 2\frac{1}{2}$　h) $1\frac{7}{8} \times \frac{4}{5}$　i) $2\frac{1}{3} \times 1\frac{3}{8}$　j) $2\frac{3}{4} \times 2\frac{1}{5}$

Division

To divide fractions you may have heard 'turn upside down and multiply'. This is what it means:

$\frac{2}{5} \div \frac{7}{8}$ has the same answer as $\frac{2}{5} \times \frac{8}{7}$

$2\frac{1}{7} \div 3$ has the same answer as $2\frac{1}{7} \times \frac{1}{3}$ [$3 = \frac{3}{1}$ as a fraction]

$2\frac{1}{7} \div 1\frac{1}{4} \rightarrow \frac{15}{7} \div \frac{5}{4}$ has the same answer as $\frac{15}{7} \times \frac{4}{5}$

Mixed numbers *must* be changed into fractions.

Finding how many eighths in $2\frac{1}{4}$ is the same as $2\frac{1}{4} \div \frac{1}{8}$ which has the same answer as $2\frac{1}{4} \times \frac{8}{1}$.

Practice 9

a) $\frac{4}{9} \div \frac{2}{3}$　　b) $\frac{4}{6} \div \frac{2}{3}$　　c) $\frac{5}{6} \div \frac{2}{9}$　　d) $3\frac{2}{3} \div 11$　e) $8 \div \frac{3}{8}$

f) $4\frac{1}{5} \div \frac{14}{15}$　g) $\frac{3}{20} \div 5\frac{1}{4}$　h) $2\frac{1}{2} \div 1\frac{3}{7}$　i) $\frac{2}{9} \div 2$　　j) $\frac{9}{10} \div 6$

Practice 10

Find how many:

a) $\frac{1}{2}$ s in $7\frac{1}{2}$　b) $\frac{1}{3}$ s in $1\frac{1}{3}$　c) $\frac{1}{4}$ s in $2\frac{1}{2}$　d) $\frac{1}{6}$ s in $1\frac{1}{2}$

Practice 11

Remember brackets tell you what to do first.

a) third of $\frac{6}{11}$　　　b) $\frac{3}{4}$ of $6\frac{1}{2}$　　　c) $(\frac{1}{2}$ of $7) + 7$

d) $4\frac{2}{3} \div 3\frac{1}{3}$　　　e) $(\frac{3}{4} + \frac{1}{2}) \times \frac{2}{15}$　　f) $1 - (\frac{1}{3} + \frac{1}{4} + \frac{1}{5})$

Fractions and Decimals

Converting decimals to fractions

Decimal numbers are a type of fraction. In fact, their proper name is *decimal fractions*. Decimal fractions can be converted into the sort of fractions you would recognise by displaying the column headings:

	U units	t tenths	h hundredths	th thousandths	
0.7→		. 7			$\rightarrow\dfrac{7}{10}$
0.008→		. 0	0	8	$\rightarrow\dfrac{8}{1000}$
0.52→		. 5	2		$\rightarrow\dfrac{52}{100}$
0.306→		. 3	0	6	$\rightarrow\dfrac{306}{1000}$
7.02→	7	. 0	2		$\rightarrow\dfrac{702}{100}$ or $7\dfrac{2}{100}$

because it's $\dfrac{5}{10}+\dfrac{2}{100}=\dfrac{50}{100}+\dfrac{2}{100}$

Some of these fractions can be simplified.

$$\frac{8}{1000}=\frac{8\div 8}{1000\div 8}=\frac{1}{125};\ \frac{52\div 4}{100\div 4}=\frac{13}{25};\ \frac{306}{1000}\ \text{and}\ 7\frac{2}{100}\ \text{can be}$$

simplified as well but $\dfrac{7}{10}$ can't be.

Practice 1

Convert these decimals into fractions in their simplest form.

a) 0.8
b) 0.45
c) 0.007
d) 0.035
e) 0.641

f) 0.73
g) 0.0026
h) 8.04
i) 11.92
j) 0.000 55

Converting fractions into decimals

Fractions can be converted into decimal numbers. Sometimes it's very quick:

	U units	.	t tenths	h hundredths	th thousandths	
$\dfrac{5}{10}\rightarrow$		.	5			→0.5
$\dfrac{59}{1000}\rightarrow$		.	0	5	9	→0.059

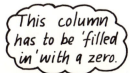

This column has to be 'filled in' with a zero.

When the fraction is not a column heading, you can think about it this way:

Example:

■ (one quarter) $\frac{1}{4}$ means $1 \div 4$, which set out as a division sum is

$$4\overline{)1.00}\;\uparrow$$

Space for more zeros, if necessary.
Before you start a calculation you often don't know how many zeros you'll need.

$$\begin{array}{r}0.25\\4\overline{)1.00}\end{array}\quad\rightarrow\quad\frac{1}{4}=0.25$$

(NB: You can now write down fractions such as $3\frac{1}{4}$ as decimals→3.25)

Further examples:

■ $\frac{3}{5}\rightarrow5\overline{)3.00}\rightarrow\begin{array}{r}0.6\\5\overline{)3.00}\\\uparrow\end{array}\rightarrow\frac{3}{5}=0.6$

unnecessary zero

■ $\frac{2}{9}\rightarrow9\overline{)2.00}\rightarrow\begin{array}{r}0.2\,2222\\9\overline{)2.^20^20000}\end{array}\quad\rightarrow\quad\frac{2}{9}=0.222\ldots$ (called 'point two recurring')

The zeros could go on forever, so could the twos.

Practice 2

Convert these fractions into decimal numbers.

a) $\frac{1}{5}$

b) $\frac{3}{4}$

c) $\frac{3}{8}$

d) $\frac{5}{6}$

e) $\frac{241}{1000}$

f) $\frac{7}{100}$

g) $\frac{1}{1\,000\,000}$ (a millionth)

h) $\frac{3}{7}$ ⎫
i) $\frac{5}{7}$ ⎬ What do you notice?

j) $\frac{2}{11}$

Comparing the size of fractions and decimals

To compare the size of a fraction and a decimal number, it is simplest to change the fraction into a decimal.

Example:

■ Which is bigger, $\frac{1}{3}$ or 0.33?

Change $\frac{1}{3}$ into decimal form:

$$\frac{1}{3}\rightarrow3\overline{)1.00}\rightarrow\begin{array}{r}0.3\,3\,33\\3\overline{)1.0^10^10^100}\end{array}\rightarrow\frac{1}{3}=0.333\text{ recurring}$$

Now compare with 0.33:

$$\frac{1}{3} = 0.33333\ldots$$

0.33

same same top line
here here bigger

$\frac{1}{3}$ is bigger than 0.33

Example:

■ Which is bigger, $\frac{1}{5}$ or 0.16?

$$\frac{1}{5} = 0.2 \text{ (practice above)}$$

Comparing with 0.16:

$$\frac{1}{5} = 0.2$$

0.16

↑

top line
bigger

$\frac{1}{5}$ is bigger than 0.16.

Practice 3

Which of the two is bigger?

a) $\frac{3}{5}$ or 0.65   d) $\frac{2}{9}$ or 0.225

b) 0.29 or $\frac{2}{7}$ e) $\frac{5}{6}$ or 0.8

c) 0.247 or $\frac{1}{4}$

Practice 4

1   What is $\frac{1}{3} + \frac{7}{9}$?
    a) $\frac{8}{12}$ b) $\frac{2}{3}$ c) $1\frac{1}{9}$ d) $\frac{8}{9}$ e) _____

2   What is $\frac{7}{8} - \frac{1}{6}$?
    a) $\frac{6}{4}$ b $\frac{5}{8}$ c) $1\frac{1}{2}$ d) $\frac{3}{4}$ e) _____

3   What is $2\frac{1}{2} - 1\frac{5}{6}$?
    a) $1\frac{1}{3}$ b) $\frac{2}{3}$ c) $\frac{4}{3}$ d) $1\frac{4}{4}$ e) _____

4   Which of these fractions is equivalent to $\frac{14}{35}$?
    a) $\frac{4}{10}$ b) $\frac{7}{20}$ c) $\frac{9}{30}$ d) $\frac{19}{40}$ e) _____

5   How many $\frac{1}{2}$s are there in 6?
    a) 12   b) 3   c) $6\frac{1}{2}$ d) 8   e) _____

6   What is $2 \div \frac{5}{6}$?
    a) $\frac{5}{12}$ b) $2\frac{2}{5}$ c) $\frac{1}{15}$ d) $\frac{3}{5}$ e) _____

7   What is $2\frac{1}{2} \times 1\frac{7}{10}$?
    a) $2\frac{7}{20}$ b) $4\frac{1}{4}$ c) $1\frac{8}{17}$ d) $1\frac{9}{10}$ e) _____

8   What is 0.075 written as a fraction in its simplest form?
    a) $\frac{75}{1000}$ b) $\frac{3}{4}$ c) $\frac{3}{40}$ d) $\frac{75}{100}$ e) _____

9   How is $\frac{7}{8}$ written as a decimal?
    a) 0.876   b) 0.87   c) 0.78   d) 114   e) _____

10   Which of these is the largest fraction?
    a) $\frac{5}{8}$ b) $\frac{3}{4}$ c) $\frac{7}{9}$ d) $\frac{8}{11}$

Percentages

Percent means 'for every hundred' or '$\frac{}{100}$'.
So 7% means $\frac{7}{100}$.

Divide by 100

The symbol % is a jumble of 100.

1 whole = 100%

Parts of a whole which are expressed as percentages have to add up to 100%.

1 whole = $\frac{100}{100}$ = 100%

Example:

■ The diagram below shows the ways heat can be lost from a house:

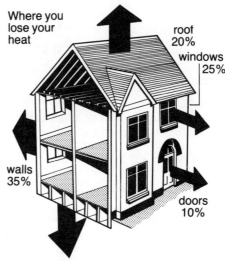

Where you lose your heat

roof 20%

windows 25%

walls 35%

doors 10%

The heat loss from the floors has been missed out. What should it be?

Roof   Windows   Doors   Walls
20%   + 25%   + 10%   + 35% = 90%   Total should be 100%.
So 100% − 90% = 10%
10% heat loss from floors.

Practice 1

Find the missing percentage in these diagrams.

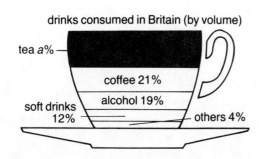

drinks consumed in Britain (by volume)

tea a%

coffee 21%

soft drinks 12%

alcohol 19%

others 4%

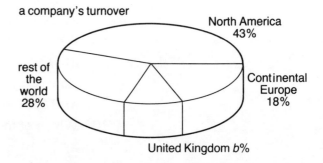

a company's turnover

North America 43%

rest of the world 28%

Continental Europe 18%

United Kingdom b%

Fractions

A percentage is just another way of expressing a fraction.

Examples:

■ $7\% = \frac{7}{100}$ which cannot be simplified. $\rightarrow 7\% = \frac{7}{100}$

■ $20\% = \frac{20}{100}$ which can be. $\rightarrow \frac{20}{100} \xrightarrow[\div 20]{\div 20} \frac{1}{5} \rightarrow 20\% = \frac{1}{5}$

■ $33\frac{1}{3}\% = \frac{33\frac{1}{3}}{100}$ and this *must* be simplified as you should have a whole number 'on top'.

$$\rightarrow \frac{33\frac{1}{3}}{100} \xrightarrow[\times 3]{\times 3} \frac{100}{300} \xrightarrow[\div 100]{\div 100} \frac{1}{3} \rightarrow 33\frac{1}{3}\% = \frac{1}{3}$$

 *Get rid of that fraction on top.*

 *Now simplify.*

Practice 2

Convert these percentages into fractions in their simplest form.

a) 25%
b) 40%
c) 9%
d) 35%
e) 72%

f) 44%
g) $12\frac{1}{2}\%$
h) $5\frac{1}{2}\%$
i) 8%
j) $92\frac{1}{2}\%$

Converting fractions

Fractions can be converted into percentages:

Examples:

■ $\frac{3}{4} \rightarrow \frac{3}{4}$ of a whole $\rightarrow \frac{3}{4}$ of 100% $\rightarrow \frac{3}{4} \times \frac{100}{1}\% = \frac{300}{4}\% \rightarrow$

$$4\overline{)30^20^20} \quad \frac{7\;5}{} \rightarrow 75\%$$

$$\rightarrow \frac{3}{4} = 75\%$$

■ Decimal fractions, too.

$0.413 \rightarrow 0.413 \times 100\% = 41.3\% \rightarrow 0.413 = 41.3\%$

Practice 3

Convert these fractions into percentages.

a) $\frac{1}{5}$

b) $\frac{7}{10}$

c) $\frac{3}{5}$

d) $\frac{1}{4}$

e) $\frac{5}{8}$

f) $\frac{7}{20}$

g) 0.57

h) 0.4

i) 0.218

j) 0.055

Comparing the size of fractions, decimals and percentages

It is simplest to convert a percentage into a decimal number in order to compare its size with a fraction or a decimal.

Example:

■ Which is the bigger, 48% or $\frac{2}{5}$?

$$48\% = \frac{48}{100} = 0.48$$

Now compare them.

$$48\% = 0.48$$

$$\frac{2}{5} = 0.40$$

↑ ↑
same top line
here bigger

$$\frac{2}{5} \rightarrow 5\overline{)2.0} \rightarrow 5\overline{)2.0}^{\,0.4} \rightarrow \frac{2}{5} = 0.4$$

48% is bigger than $\frac{2}{5}$

Practice 4

Which is bigger?
a) $\frac{1}{10}$ or 9%?

b) $\frac{3}{8}$ or 37%?

c) $\frac{3}{4}$ or 75%?

d) $\frac{5}{6}$ or 90%?

e) $\frac{2}{3}$ or 65%?

Practice 5

Write these in order of size, smallest first:
a) $\frac{2}{3}$, 66%, 0.65

b) 0.95 $\frac{1}{10}$, 9%

c) 0.09, 10%, $\frac{1}{8}$

d) 22%, $\frac{1}{5}$, 0.219

e) $\frac{1}{2}$, 49%, 0.5062

Percentages of amounts

Examples:

■ What is 20% of 455 g?

20% = $\frac{1}{5}$ (see earlier section)

20% of 455 = $\frac{1}{5}$ of 455 = $\frac{1}{5}$ × 455 = 91

So 20% of 455 g = 91 g

■ What is 35% of 600 ml?

$$35\% = \frac{35}{100} = \frac{7}{20}$$

35% of 600 = $\frac{7}{20}$ of 600 = $\frac{7}{20}$ × 600 = 210

So 35% of 600 ml = 210 ml

Practice 6

Calculate the following amounts:
a) 20% of 65 ml
b) 50% of 350 g
c) 45% of 140 ml
d) 35% of 40 tons
e) 5% of 27 g

More percentages

Example:

■ A can of cola normally contains 440 ml. It advertises 20% extra free. How much does it now contain?

$20\% = \frac{1}{5}$

20% of $440 = \frac{1}{5}$ of $440 = \frac{1}{5} \times 440 = 88$

20% of 440 ml $= 88$ ml

So the can now contains $440 + 88 = 528$ ml.

Practice 7

The following table shows a number of products being promoted by giving the customer some extra amount free. Copy and complete the table.

	Product	Usual size	Percent extra	Promotion size
a)	Shaving foam	200 g	20%	?
b)	Dental floss	50 m	10%	?
c)	Hair conditioner	240 ml	20%	?
d)	Talcum powder	150 g	30%	?
e)	Bath cleaner	215 ml	20%	?
f)	Shampoo	150 ml	20%	?
g)	Skin cleanser	100 ml	?	125 ml
h)	Lavatory cleaner	?	20%	600 ml
i)	Sting relief cream	?	10%	22 g
j)	Bath salts	750 g	?	825 g

Accuracy and Approximations

Estimation

Exaggeration

Most people use numbers in their everyday life, often at work. A bank clerk has to be able to account for every penny passing through her or his till. In a stocktake every item of stock has to be recorded.

Often, though, when using numbers it is not always necessary to be totally accurate. A newspaper report of a football match may give the crowd size to the nearest thousand fans, and that would be acceptable to most readers.

Sometimes it is not possible to be exact. For instance, *all* measurements are approximate. However precise you try to make a measurement, there will always be better equipment that would make a more accurate one. So when you make a measurement, you should always think: 'How accurate does this need to be?' When measuring a room for decoration it is probably only necessary to work to the nearest foot or metre. However, the glass for a window frame needs to be measured to the nearest millimetre. An atomic scientist makes measurements to millionths of millimetres.

For these reasons it is very important to understand how to approximate correctly.

Rounding to nearest whole number

Prices in shops are often given as so many pounds and, say, 99p or 95p. When thinking about the cost it is tempting to knock off the 'odd' pence, but really they're not so 'odd' at all. They nearly make a whole extra pound. So, £124.99 is £125 to the nearest pound. And £299.95 is £300 to the nearest pound.

Any decimal number can be rounded to the nearest whole unit. You have to decide, by looking at the decimal part, whether the number is nearest the next whole number up or down. There is a simple way of doing this:

units tenths
  ↘   ↙   (correct
12.367 is 12   to nearest whole
                         number)

This is called rounding down.

tenths
   ↓   (correct
8.87 is 9   to nearest whole
                       number)

This is called rounding up.

The rule is:
Look at the tenths and

| 0 | 1 | 2 | 3 | 4 | | 5 | 6 | 7 | 8 | 9 |

round down   round-up

Practice 1

Round these amounts correct to the nearest whole unit.
a) 12.33   d) £36.49
b) 4.6242   e) £7.89
c) 100.8   f) 0.72

Other whole number approximations

You can make approximations to the nearest thousand, or hundred, or million, depending on the circumstances.

A football crowd of 29 243 might be reported as a gate of 29 000 in the local paper.

In the 1981 census, the population of Avon was recorded as 915 176. That's 1 million (to the nearest million).

Here's how you do it.

thousands

29②43 is 29 000 (to nearest thousand)
↑
Look at this
figure.

million
↓
⑨15 176
↑
Look at this → Round up, → 1 000 000
figure.   from zero   **to one**
           millions   **million**

9	
8	
7	round
6	up
5	
4	
3	round
2	down
1	
0	

99 to nearest ten

  T   T
9⑨ → round up → 100 (ten tens!)
 ↑
Look at this
figure.

Practice 2

Round these numbers:
a) 34 422 (to nearest thousand)
b) 99 (to nearest hundred)
c) 104 (to nearest hundred)
d) 256 (to nearest ten)
e) 999 (to nearest ten)
f) 207 644 (to nearest ten thousand)

Significant figures

Rounding correctly to a given number of significant figures is done like this:
First count your significant figures from the left.
The rest of the number is then rounded.

Examples:

■ Round 29 243 to 1 significant figure

Look at this figure.
↓
→ 2⑨243
↑   ↘
the significant round up
figure   ↘

30 000

The significant figures are the most important figures...

But you can't really say those end zeros are not important.

■ Round 29 243 to 3 significant figures

→ 29 2④3 → round down → 292 000
  ↑
the significant
figures

■ Round 999 to 2 significant figures
→ 99⑨ → round up → 1000
   ↑   ↑
the significant   These are now the
figures   significant figures.

This type of rounding can be done to decimal numbers as well:

Round 4.5927 to 2 significant figures.

→4.5⑨27→round up→4.6

↑

the significant
figures

Round 0.00542 to 1 significant figure.

→0.005④2→round down→0.005

↑

the significant
figure

Practice 3

Round these numbers:
a) 362 (to 2 significant figures)
b) 5632 (to 1 significant figure)
c) 99 (to 1 significant figure)
d) 3.6245 (to 3 significant figures)
e) 456.62 (to 3 significant figures)
f) 19.892 (to 2 significant figures)
g) 0.0344 (to 2 significant figures)

Decimal places

Decimals can be rounded correct to a given number of decimal places.

This is very similar to what we've done before with whole numbers because rounding to two decimal places, say, is the same as rounding to the nearest hundredth.

Round 4.5927 to 2 decimal places.

→4.59②7→round down→4.59

↑

2 decimal
places

Round 0.005 42 to 2 decimal places.

→6.00⑤42→round up→0.01

↑

2 decimal places

Round 0.004 52 to 2 decimal places.

→0.00④52→round down→0.00   zero!

When carrying out calculations on money, working to the nearest penny means working to 2 decimal places if pounds are involved. 1p = £0.01

Example:

■ Three children are given £5 between them by their grandmother. How much do they each get?

$$£5 \div 3 \rightarrow £5.00 \div 3 \rightarrow \quad 3\overline{)5.{}^20{}^20\,00}\ldots$$

1. 6 666   this recurs

↑↑

1.6666 . . . to 2 decimal places→1.66⑥6→round up→1.67
Answer = £1.67 each

Practice 4	Round these numbers as directed:
	a) 6.207 (to 2 decimal places)
	b) 0.1557 (to 3 decimal places)
	c) 12.822 (to 1 decimal place)
	d) 0.007 (to 1 decimal place)

Practice 5	Work out:
	a) $60 \div 7$ (answer to 2 decimal places)
	b) $53 \div 3$ (answer to 3 significant figures)
	c) $2697 \div 5$ (answer to 2 significant figures)
	d) 57×63 (answer to the nearest hundred)
	e) 2 kg of soap powder cost £2.89. How much is this for one kg to the nearest penny?
	f) Seven people in a syndicate win £122.54 on the pools. How much do they each get?

Practice 6	Write down these figures:
	a) 2507 correct to the nearest thousand
	b) 14.243 correct to 3 significant figures
	c) 7.635 correct to nearest whole number
	d) 96 correct to 1 significant figure
	e) 0.432 correct to nearest whole number
	f) 2392 correct to 2 significant figures
	g) 0.003 61 correct to 3 decimal places
	h) 0.003 61 correct to 1 decimal place
	i) 996 correct to 2 significant figures
	j) 523 496 correct to nearest ten thousand

Length and Weight

Made to measure

Two systems dominate our measurements today. They are the *metric system* and the *imperial system*. The metric system, or *Système International (SI)*, is gradually replacing the imperial system in this country. In the rest of Europe only the metric system is used, but in the United States the imperial system is in full use. So it is important to be able to understand and use both systems.

Length in the imperial system

The longest measure of length is the mile and the smallest, the inch (in). In between measures are the foot (ft) and the yard (yd).

$\times 12$	**You need to remember**	$\times 3$
feet → inches	12 inches = 1 foot	yards → feet
← $\div 12$	3 feet = 1 yard 1760 yards = 1 mile	← $\div 3$

Examples:

◼ How many inches in 2 yards?

1 yd = 3 ft
∴ 2 yds = 6 ft
1 ft = 12 ins
6 × 12 = 72
6 ft = 72 ins
2 yd = 72 ins

◼ Express 54 inches in feet and inches.

12 ins = 1 ft
54 ÷ 12 = 4 remainder 6
54 ins = 4 ft 6 ins

Metric length

The metric system is a decimal system. The jumps between units are in tens, hundreds or thousands. The basic unit of length is the metre.

<table>
<tr><td>× 10
──→
cm   mm
←──
÷ 10</td><td>**You need to remember**
1000 millimetres (mm) = 1 metre
100 centimetres (cm) = 1 metre
10 millimetres = 1 centimetre
1000 metres = 1 kilometre (km)</td><td>× 100
──→
metre   cm
←──
÷ 100</td></tr>
<tr><td>× 1000
──→
km   metre
←──
÷ 1000</td><td>*kilo* means a thousand
milli means a thousandth</td><td>× 1000
──→
metre   mm
←──
÷ 1000</td></tr>
</table>

Examples:

◼ How many metres are there in 7 km?

1 km = 1000 m
7 × 1000 = 7000
7 km = 7000 m

◼ Convert 79 mm into centimetres.

10 mm = 1 cm
79 ÷ 10 = 7.9
79 mm = 7.9 cm

◼ Write these lengths in order of size, smallest first: 295 mm, 0.186 m, 30 cm.

Change all the measurements to the same units, mm will do.

0.186 m = 0.186 × 1000 mm = 186 mm
30 cm = 30 × 10 mm = 300 mm
So, in order of size, we have 186 mm, 295 mm, 300 mm.
That is, 0.186 m, 295 mm, 30 cm.

■ What is the length x in the diagram?

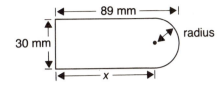

The semicircle is 30 mm across. So it has radius 15 mm.
Therefore, the length x is $89 - 15 = 74$ mm.

Practice 1

Convert these measurements into the units given:
a) 56 mm into centimetres
b) 6.5 km into metres
c) 2 ft 5 ins into inches
d) 566 cm into metres
e) 4 miles into yards
f) 7 yds 2 ft into feet
g) 2566 mm into metres

Practice 2

Put these lengths in order of size (smallest first):
a) 62 ins, 5 ft, 2 yds
b) 1.5 km, 1876 mm, 220 cm

Practice 3

Work out the length of the side indicated:

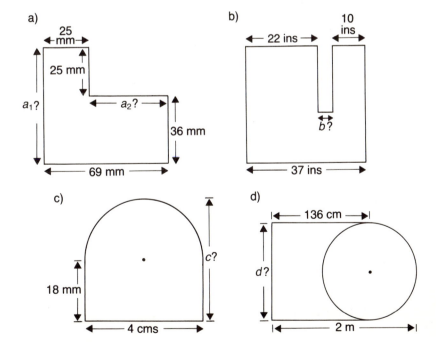

Weight

In the imperial system, weight is measured in *ounces* (oz), *pounds* (lb), *stones, hundredweight* (cwt), and *tons*.

	You need to remember	
$\xrightarrow{\times 16}$ pounds ounces $\xleftarrow{\div 16}$	16 oz = 1 lb 14 lb = 1 stone 112 lb = 1 cwt 20 cwt = 1 ton	$\xrightarrow{\times 14}$ stones pounds $\xleftarrow{\div 14}$

Examples:

■ Change 3 lbs into ounces.

1 lb = 16 oz
$3 \times 16 = 48$
3 lbs = 48 oz

■ A child weighs 6 stone 5 lbs. How many pounds is this?

1 stone = 14 lbs
6 stone = 6×14 lbs = 84 lbs
so, 6 stone 5 lbs = $84 + 5 = 89$ lbs.

The basic unit of weight in the metric system is the *gram* (g).

	You need to remember	
$\xrightarrow{\times 1000}$ kilogram gram $\xleftarrow{\div 1000}$	1000 g = 1 kilogram (kg) 1000 kg = 1 tonne	$\xrightarrow{\times 1000}$ tonne kg $\xleftarrow{\div 1000}$

Example:

■ Express 2300 g in kilogram.

$2300 \div 1000 = 2.300$
$\therefore$ 2300 g = 2.3 kg

Practice 4

Change these weights into the units given:
a) 10 stone into pounds
b) 2.2 kg into grams
c) 2300 kg into tonnes
d) 230 g into kilograms
e) 9 tons into hundredweight
f) 1 ton into pounds
   Approximately how many pounds is 1 tonne = 1000 kg?

Longer Problems (A)

1 The table below shows the tariffs for the Isle of Wight car ferry. Two adults and a child are travelling with their car, a Rover 200 saloon (length 4.16 metres), during the winter months.
   a) What fraction of the adult single fare is the child's single fare?
   b) What is the cost of a single journey for this group?
   c) How much would they save if they take a mid-week return for the car rather than pay for two lots of single journeys?

Car Ferry Tariffs

		Single	Return
Motorists' Fares		£	£
(Drivers and accompanying passengers)			
Adult		1.78	3.56
Child (5 but under 16)		0.89	1.78
Dog (accompanying passenger)		0.89	1.78
Bicycle (accompanying passenger)		FREE	FREE

The new m.v. St. Catherine

Vehicle Rates

	Single	Wight Night Single	Midweek Return	3 Day Return	All-in Day Excursion
			Reduced Winter Rates 1 January to 14 April and 7 October to 31 December		
	(see note 1)	(see note 2)	(see note 3)	(see note 4)	(see note 5)
Cars & Motorised Caravans Overall length	£	£	£	£	£
Not exceeding 4.00m	8.05	4.85	13.70	12.10	16.00
Not exceeding 5.50m	10.70	6.45	18.20	16.10	16.00
Exceeding 5.50m, per additional metre or part thereof	1.95	1.20	3.30	3.00	—

2 This pie chart shows a breakdown of criminal offences for the year 1985.
   a) Looking at the pie chart, estimate what *fraction* of the crimes committed were burglary? Was it i) $\frac{1}{8}$, ii) $\frac{1}{4}$ or iii) $\frac{5}{8}$?
   b) *Calculate* the exact percentage of crimes which were burglary?
   c) Express 15% as a fraction in its simplest form.

There were approximately $3\frac{1}{2}$ million offences recorded by the police in 1985.
   d) Write $3\frac{1}{2}$ million in figures.
   e) What number were criminal damage?

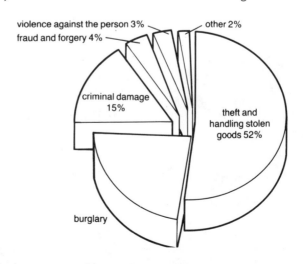

1985

3 A national company advertises that it employs 23% of its 44 000 workforce in the South and 38% in Wales and the Midlands. The rest are employed in the North and Scotland.
a) What percentage are employed in the North and Scotland?
b) 16 720 people are employed in Wales and the Midlands. How many people is this, correct to two significant figures?
c) How many people are employed in the South?
d) 12 100 of the employees are women. What percentage of the company's workforce is this?

4 Letter post is charged within Britain at the following rates:

Letter Post

Weight not over	1st class	2nd class	Weight not over	1st class	2nd class
60g	18p	13p	500g	92p	70p
100g	26p	20p	600g	£1.15	85p
150g	32p	24p	700g	£1.35	£1.00
200g	40p	30p	750g	£1.45	£1.05
250g	48p	37p	800g	£1.55	Not admissible over 750g
300g	56p	43p	900g	£1.70	
350g	64p	49p	1000g	£1.85	
400g	72p	55p	Each extra 250g or part thereof 45p		
450g	82p	62p			

a) How much does it cost to send a letter weighing 70 g, by first class post?
b) How much more expensive is it to send a 350 g package by first class letter post than by second class post?
c) A 100 g item costs 20p second class and 26p first class. What is the percentage *extra* cost to send the item by first rather than second class post?
d) A person wants to send a single package by letter post containing items with weights 800 g, 250 g, 200 g and 50 g. What will this cost to post?

5 A vacuum cleaner uses 1 unit of electricity in $1\frac{1}{2}$ hour's use.
a) Express $1\frac{1}{2}$ as a proper fraction.
b) How much electricity, in units, is used by a vacuum cleaner in 1 hour?
c) Electricity costs 5.32p per unit. How much does it cost to run a vacuum cleaner for 3 hours?

Money

In this chapter, and the next, we look at some calculations involving money.

Hire Purchase (HP).

Hire Purchase is a way that you can buy something from a shop, like a television or a stereo unit, and not pay for it all at once. Instead you pay gradually in instalments, usually once a month. The shop arranges with a finance company to supply the money for a purchase and you, the customer, repay the finance company. The total repayment has to be more than the original cost of the goods, otherwise the finance company would make no profit. HP is used for large purchases (you can't buy jeans or records on HP), and technically the finance company owns the goods until you have paid off the debt in full.

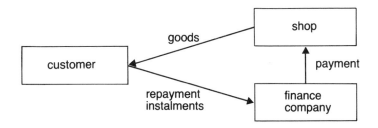

To buy something on HP you have to fill out quite a long application form. It will include personal details and a section like this:

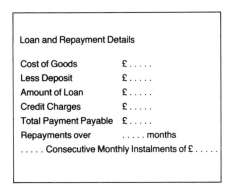

example: buying a colour TV on HP

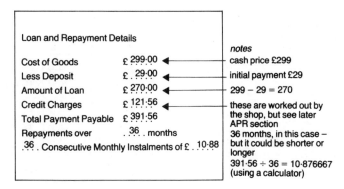

47

Practice 1

Make ten copies of the loan and repayment form and complete them for the following purchases:

Item	Cash price	Deposit	Credit charges	Number of Repayments
a) Camera	£119.99	£12	£40.57	24
b) Microwave	£219	no deposit	£75.48	24
c) Sports cycle	£129.99	£13	£25.52	12
d) Hifi midi system	£319.99	£32	£115.63	36
e) Portable colour TV	£199.99	£20	£50.42	12
f) Home computer	£159.99	no deposit	£50.36	24
g) Mechanics tool kit	£89.95	no deposit	£21.20	12
h) Greenhouse	£199.99	£20	£75.82	24
i) Electric sewing machine	£119.95	£20	£20.63	12
j) Electric lead guitar	£99.99	no deposit	£31.46	24

Bank loans

Another important way of buying something without having to pay cash immediately is to take out a *personal loan* from a bank. The bank will want to know what you intend to buy, and may make conditions or even refuse the loan. If the bank agrees to make the loan, it will transfer the money to your current account. Then you can make your purchase, paying for it with a cheque.

Below is a table showing the repayments you would have to make if you borrowed money from a bank.

Personal loan repayment tables

amount	12 months annual percentage rate of charge 19.62%			24 months annual percentage rate of charge 19.82%			36 months annual percentage rate of charge 19.47%		
	total interest	monthly payment	total amount payable	total interest	monthly payment	total amount payable	total interest	monthly payment	total amount payable
£	£	£	£	£	£	£	£	£	£
10	1.04	0.92	11.04	2.00	0.50	12.00	2.96	0.36	12.96
20	1.96	1.83	21.96	4.00	1.00	24.00	5.92	0.72	25.92
30	3.00	2.75	33.00	6.00	1.50	36.00	8.88	1.08	38.88
40	4.04	3.67	44.04	8.00	2.00	48.00	11.84	1.44	51.84
50	4.96	4.58	54.96	10.00	2.50	50.00	15.16	1.81	95.16
60	6.00	5.50	66.00	12.00	3.00	72.00	18.12	2.17	78.12
70	7.04	5.42	77.04	14.00	3.50	84.00	21.08	2.53	91.08
80	7.96	7.33	87.96	16.00	4.00	96.00	24.04	2.89	104.04
90	9.00	9.25	99.00	18.00	4.50	108.00	27.00	3.25	117.00
100	10.04	9.17	110.04	20.00	5.00	120.00	29.96	3.61	129.96
200	19.96	18.33	219.96	40.00	10.00	240.00	59.92	7.22	259.92
300	30.00	27.50	330.00	60.00	15.00	360.00	89.88	10.83	389.88
400	40.04	36.67	440.04	90.00	20.00	480.00	119.84	14.44	519.84
500	49.96	45.83	549.96	100.00	25.00	600.00	150.16	18.06	650.16
600	60.00	55.00	660.00	120.00	30.00	720.00	180.12	21.67	780.12
700	70.04	64.17	770.04	140.00	35.00	840.00	210.08	25.28	910.08
800	79.96	73.33	879.96	160.00	40.00	960.00	240.04	28.89	1040.04
900	90.00	82.50	990.00	180.00	45.00	1080.00	270.00	32.50	1170.00
1000	100.04	91.67	1100.04	200.00	50.00	1200.00	299.96	36.11	1299.96
2000	199.96	183.33	2199.96	400.00	100.00	2400.00	599.92	72.22	2599.92
3000	300.00	275.00	3300.00	500.00	150.00	3600.00	899.88	108.33	3899.88
4000	400.04	366.67	4400.04	800.00	200.00	4800.00	1199.84	144.44	5199.84
5000	499.96	458.33	5499.96	1000.00	250.00	6000.00	1500.16	180.56	6500.16

Examples:

- A loan of £500 over 36 months will require repayments of £18.06 per month. This includes a total of £150.16 in loan interest.
- To calculate the repayments on a loan of £1860 over 24 months you have to break it down to loans of £1000, £800 and £60. Then you add up the repayments for each:

Loan £	Repayments over 24 months £
1000	50.00
800	40.00
60	3.00
1860	93.00

Total amount payable £
1200
960
72
2232

Practice 2

Calculate the monthly repayments for these loans. What is the total amount payable in each case?
a) £400 over 36 months
b) £550 over 12 months
c) £1040 over 36 months
d) £2310 over 24 months
e) £1960 over 24 months

Cost of loans and the APR

It is often difficult to tell which is the cheapest way to borrow money. However, loan companies are now obliged to tell you the APR of a loan. This stands for the *Annual Percentage Rate* and is the percentage cost of a loan calculated over a year. So, for example, 28% APR means that a loan of £100 would cost £28 if you paid it all back a year later. The smaller the APR, the cheaper the cost of the loan. A loan at 34.2% APR is more expensive than one at 28% APR.

More Money

Percentages of money

Percentages of money are quite easy to work out because 1% of £1 is 1 pence. From this starting point you can work out other percentages of different amounts.

Example:

■ What is 8% of £23?

$$1\% \text{ of } £23 = 23p$$
$$\text{So } 8\% \text{ of } £23 = 8 \times 23p = 184p = £1.84$$

Practice 1

Calculate these amounts:

a) 5% of £35

b) 9% of £26

c) 7% of £126

d) 15% of £60

e) 30% of £45.60

f) 4% of £25

g) 8% of £11.50

h) 25% of £5.20

i) 75% of £17.60

j) 40% of £9.62

Percentage deposit

In Practice 1 of the last chapter you were given the deposit required in various HP deals. This will probably have been calculated from a percentage of the original cash price.

Example:

■ A leading chain of photographic stores requires 10% deposit.
What is 10% of a camera's cash price of £119.99?

10% of £119.99
1% of £119.99 = 119.99p
(NB: You can't really have .99p.)
So   10% of £119.99 = 10 × 119.99p = 1199.9p
      = 1200p (to nearest whole pence)
      = £12

Practice 2

Find the deposit on these items:

	Price	Deposit
a) Microwave	£219	10%
b) Sports cycle	£130	20%
c) Home computer	£160	15%
d) Mechanics tool kit	£90	5%
e) Greenhouse	£200	$12\frac{1}{2}\%$
f) Electric sewing machine	£120	8%

Value Added Tax (VAT)

Value Added Tax is what is known as an *indirect tax*. This is because it taxes people on what they buy instead of what they earn. If you don't buy anything you don't pay any of this sort of tax. Food and some other basic necessities are not taxed, but almost everything else you buy is. VAT applies to services as well. This means that food from a takeaway is taxed because a service has been done in cooking it.

The standard rate of VAT at the moment is 15%. Most shops now simply include VAT in the price they display on the goods. Some shops, garages and restaurants add it on as a separate item on the bill.

Example:

■ A typewriter ribbon costs £3.75 plus VAT at 15%. What is its total cost?

1% of £3.75 is 3.75p
15% of £3.75 is 15 × 3.75p = 56.25p = 56p (to nearest penny)
The price including VAT is therefore £3.75 + 56p = £4.31.

Practice 3

What will these prices be when VAT is added?
a) £3.00
b) £4.60
c) £1.50
d) £2.36
e) 90p
f) £83
g) £142
h) £65.50
i) £25.45
j) £16.73

Discounts

The most common way of giving a discount is to take a percentage off the price.

Example:

■ A hi-fi shop offers 5% discount to students. A cassette deck costs £95.80. What is the price after discount?

The discount will be 5% of £95.80.
1% of £95.80 is 95.80p
5% of £95.80 is 5 × 95.80p = 479p = £4.79
The discounted price is therefore £95.80 − £4.79 = £91.01.

Practice 4

What is the price of these items after discount?

	Price	Discount
a) Hi-fi midi system	£320	5%
b) Portable colour TV	£200	5%
c) Haircut	£6.50	10%
d) Jeans	£17.50	10%
e) Rail ticket	£26.40	25%
f) Dry cleaning bill	£4.32	10%

51

Simple Interest

Interest taken for a loan or given on money invested or saved is usually calculated as a percentage of the amounts involved. There are various ways of doing this. *Simple Interest* is, as its name implies, the easiest method.

You must beware when comparing interest rates. You can generally compare two interest rates only if they are both expressed as APRs, mentioned in the last chapter.

However, back to simple interest:

8% per annum (p.a.) simple interest on £120 is £9.60 each year (that's what per annum means). (Check that 8% of £120 = £9.60).

The interest payable on a £120 loan over 2 years at 8% p.a. is
$$£9.60 \times 2 = £19.20$$

There is a formula which can be used to work out simple interest. It is:

$$I = \frac{PRT}{100}$$

I is the amount of interest
R is the percentage rate (in this example it's 8)
P is the principal, the amount on which the interest is calculated (£120)
T is the length of time (2 years)

So we'd have:
$$I = 120 \times 8 \times 2 \div 100 = 960 \times 2 \div 100 = 1920 \div 100 = 19.20$$
$$\text{Interest is £19.20}$$

Practice 5

Using the formula $I = \frac{PRT}{100}$

Calculate the amounts of interest on these principals:

	Principal	Interest Rate (p.a.)	Period
a)	£200	8%	2 years
b)	£2950	8%	5 years
c)	£155	10%	2 years
d)	£820	10%	3 years
e)	£450	12%	$1\frac{1}{2}$ years
f)	£3200	15%	3 years
g)	£120	$12\frac{1}{2}$ %	1 year
h)	£625	8%	3 years

In your head

There are many occasions when it is useful to be able to do calculations in your head (and not just when doing a mental arithmetic test!). For instance, you can't really get out a calculator or pen and paper to check your change in a shop. Here are a few tips to help you get answers quickly and accurately to the kind of sums you might have to do when shopping.

Examples:

■ Take 26p away from £1
or
What change should you get from £1 if you spend 26p?

Count it out in your head like this:

26p→30p→40p→50p→60p→70p→80p→90p→£1

4p   70p

altogether <u>74p</u> change

■ What change do you get from a £5 note if you spend £2.73?

Work this out in the same way:
£2.73→£2.80→£2.90→£3→£4→£5

7p   20p   £2

altogether <u>£2.27</u> change

■ What is the total cost of three items at £1.99 each?

£1.99 is £2 less 1p
$3 \times £1.99$ is $3 \times £2$ less $3 \times 1p$
$= £6$ less 3p
Total cost $= $ <u>£5.97</u>

■ Ten children share £1.70 equally between them. How much do they each get?

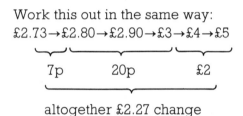

£1.70 = 170p
170p ÷ 10 = 17p
They get 17p each.

■ 10% discount is offered by a shop. What discount is there on an item costing £1.70?

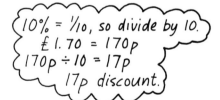

10% = ¹⁄₁₀, so divide by 10.
£1.70 = 170p
170p ÷ 10 = 17p
17p discount.

■ VAT is levied at 15% of cost. What is the VAT on something costing £1.70?

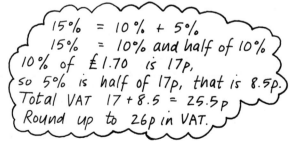

15% = 10% + 5%
15% = 10% and half of 10%
10% of £1.70 is 17p,
so 5% is half of 17p, that is 8.5p.
Total VAT 17 + 8.5 = 25.5p
Round up to 26p in VAT.

It is often very easy to work out percentages of amounts of money starting from 10%, then 20% is double, 5% half, 15% = 10% + 5% and so on.

Practice 6

Work these out in your head:
a) You spend 56p. What is the change from £1?
b) You spend £2.73. What is the change from a ten pound note?
c) You buy 3 lb of potatoes at 7p per lb. What is the total cost?
d) You buy a cup of tea for 20p and a coffee for 27p. How much change from 50p?
e) A dozen eggs cost £1.20. How much is this for each egg?
f) What is the cost of seven records at 99p each?
g) What is 5% of £1.20?
h) What is 15% of £1.20?
i) How much do 4 metres of material cost at £2.95 per metre?
j) A pair of shoes is reduced by 40% in a sale. The original price was £30. What is the sale price?

Area and Perimeter

Perimeter

The *perimeter* of a shape is the distance around it. It is easy to find the perimeter of shapes such as rectangles, squares and triangles. You simply add the lengths of the sides. As perimeter is a length, it has length units, such as metres, feet, miles and so on.

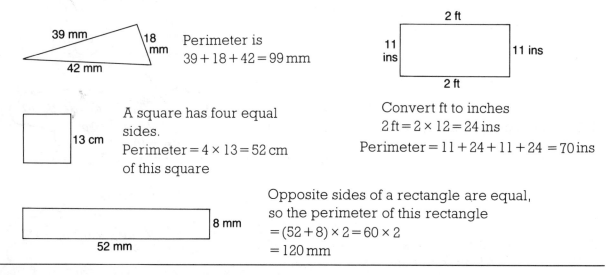

Perimeter is
$39 + 18 + 42 = 99$ mm

Convert ft to inches
$2 \text{ ft} = 2 \times 12 = 24 \text{ ins}$
Perimeter $= 11 + 24 + 11 + 24 = 70 \text{ ins}$

A square has four equal sides.
Perimeter $= 4 \times 13 = 52$ cm of this square

Opposite sides of a rectangle are equal, so the perimeter of this rectangle
$= (52 + 8) \times 2 = 60 \times 2$
$= 120$ mm

Practice 1

Give the perimeter of the following figures:
a) triangle with sides 8 cm, 12 cm and 15 cm
b) triangle with sides 2 cm, 7 mm and 0.025 mm
c) rectangle, 7 ft by 7 ins
d) square with sides 8 m
e) rectangle, 1 m by 56 cm

Practice 2

Different shapes can have the same perimeter. Which pairs of shapes have the same perimeter?

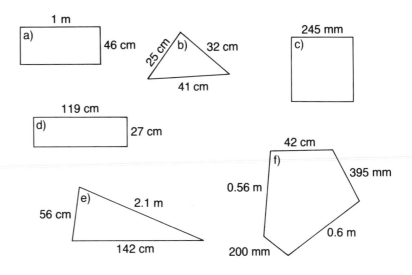

Circumference

For shapes which do not have straight sides, finding the perimeter is more of a problem. One method is to put string around the shape, then straighten the string before measuring it.

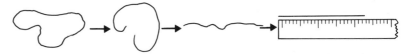

If you try this method on circles, you'd find that the perimeter, or *circumference* – the special word for the perimeter of a circle – is about three times the diameter (*d*).

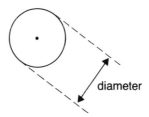

The formula for the circumference (*C*) of a circle is:

$$C = \pi \times d$$

π (pronounced 'pie') is a special number which cannot be written down exactly in figures. Its value is:

$\pi = 3.141\ 59$ (and these decimals go on for ever and ever)

$\pi = 3$ is a reasonable approximation. $\pi = 3.1$ and $\pi = \frac{22}{7}$ are better approximations. In maths questions you will be told what approximation to use. In real life you have to decide depending on the level of accuracy you are working to.

Examples:

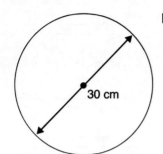

■ **Circumference**

$= 3.14 \times 30$

$= 94.2 \, cm$

(take $\pi = 3.14$)

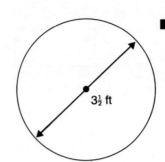

■ **Circumference**

$= 3\frac{1}{2} \times \frac{22}{7}$ $\quad (3\frac{1}{2} = \frac{7}{2})$

$= \frac{7}{2} \times \frac{\overset{11}{\cancel{22}}}{\cancel{7}}$

$= 11 \, ft$

(take $\pi = \dfrac{22}{7}$)

It is sometimes easier to work out the circumference of a circle from its *radius*. The radius is exactly half the diameter. In other words the diameter (d) is twice the radius (r), $d = 2 \times r$.

Practice 3

Copy and complete the following table:

	radius	diameter
a)	52 cm	. . .
b)	9 ins	. . .
c)	. . . mm	26 mm
d)	. . . cm	37 cm
e)	. . . ins	1 yd

The formula for the circumference (C) of a circle is:

$$C = 2\pi r = 2 \times \pi \times r$$

Example:

■

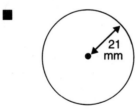

(take $\pi = \dfrac{22}{7}$)

$\text{circumference} = 2 \times \dfrac{22}{7} \times 21$

$= 2 \times \dfrac{22}{7} \times \overset{3}{\cancel{21}}$

$= 44 \times 3$

$= 132 \, mm.$

Practice 4

Find the circumference of these circles:
a) radius 3 cm (take $\pi = 3.14$)
b) radius 7 ft (take $\pi = \frac{22}{7}$)
c) radius 4.9 m (take $\pi = \frac{22}{7}$, and write 4.9 as $\frac{49}{10}$)
d) radius 24.7 mm take $\pi = 3.1$)
e) diameter 35 yds (take $\pi = \frac{22}{7}$)

f)

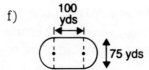

100 yds

75 yds

A running track is shown in the diagram. What is the total distance around the track? (take $\pi = 3.1$)

Area

Area is the amount of surface covered by a shape. Imagine the shape covering a grid of squares that are all the same size. You could measure the area of the shape by counting up the squares it covered. So area is measured in square units, such as square centimetres (cm^2). $1\ cm^2$ is the area covered by a square with sides 1 cm. Other units such as square feet (ft^2) and square metres (m^2) are set in the same way.

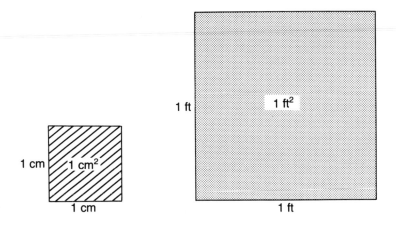

The area of simple shapes, such as rectangles and squares, can easily be found:

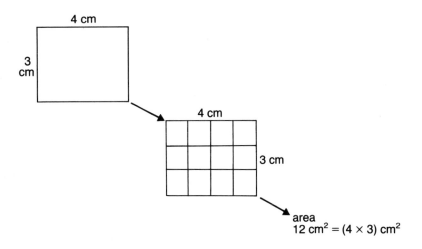

You multiply the base length by the height. But both measurements *must* be in the same units.

Example:

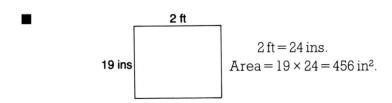

2 ft = 24 ins.
Area = $19 \times 24 = 456\ in^2$.

Find the area of these rectangles and squares:

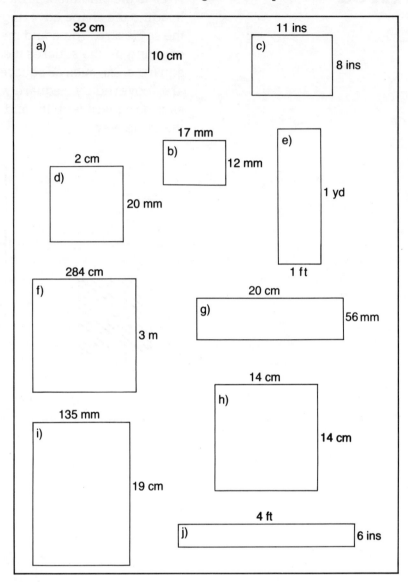

Example:

■ The area of some shapes can be found by splitting the shape into rectangles:

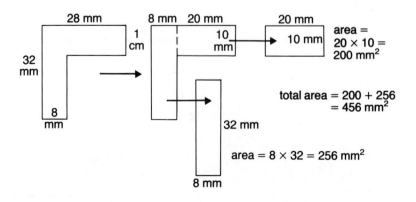

Find the area of these shapes:

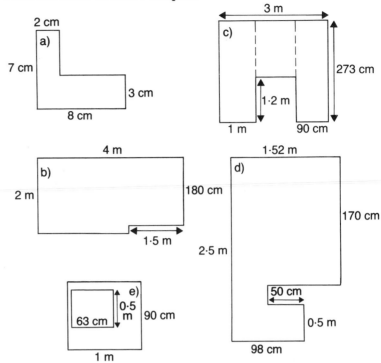

The area of triangles

All triangles can be looked at like this:

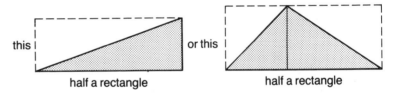

this | half a rectangle | or this | half a rectangle

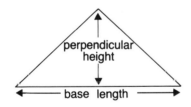

So, the area of a triangle is:

$$A = \frac{1}{2} \times \text{area of rectangle}$$
$$A = \frac{1}{2} \times \text{base length} \times \text{perpendicular height}$$
$$A = \frac{1}{2} \times b \times h$$

Examples:

■ Area $= \frac{1}{2} \times 7 \times 3$

$\qquad = \frac{1}{2} \times 21$

$\qquad = 10\frac{1}{2}$ cm²

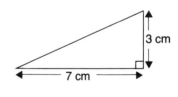

■ Area $= \frac{1}{2} \times 40 \times 28$

$\qquad = 20 \times 28$

$\qquad = 560$ mm²

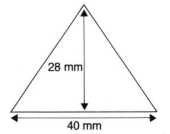

59

Practice 7

Find the area of these triangles:

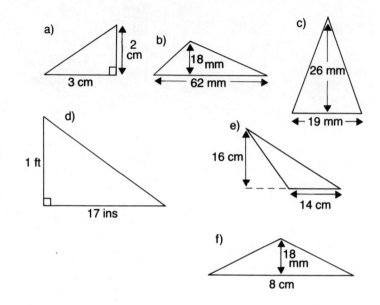

a) 2 cm, 3 cm

b) 18 mm, 62 mm

c) 26 mm, 19 mm

d) 1 ft, 17 ins

e) 16 cm, 14 cm

f) 18 mm, 8 cm

Circles

The area of a circle is given by the formula $A = \pi r^2$, which means $\pi \times r \times r$ (r is the circle's radius and π is that number which cannot be written down exactly.)

Examples:

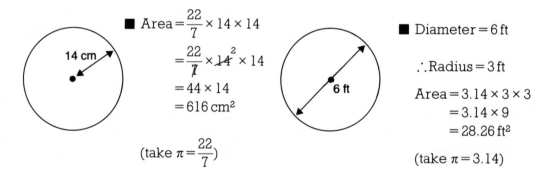

■ Area $= \dfrac{22}{7} \times 14 \times 14$

$= \dfrac{22}{\cancel{7}} \times \cancel{14}^{2} \times 14$

$= 44 \times 14$

$= 616 \text{ cm}^2$

14 cm

(take $\pi = \dfrac{22}{7}$)

■ Diameter $= 6\,\text{ft}$

∴ Radius $= 3\,\text{ft}$

Area $= 3.14 \times 3 \times 3$

$= 3.14 \times 9$

$= 28.26 \text{ ft}^2$

6 ft

(take $\pi = 3.14$)

Practice 8

Find the area of these circles:

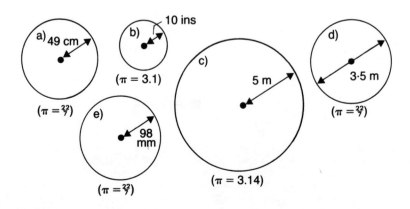

a) 49 cm ($\pi = \frac{22}{7}$)

b) 10 ins ($\pi = 3.1$)

c) 5 m ($\pi = 3.14$)

d) 3·5 m ($\pi = \frac{22}{7}$)

e) 98 mm ($\pi = \frac{22}{7}$)

Find the perimeter and/or area of these shapes:

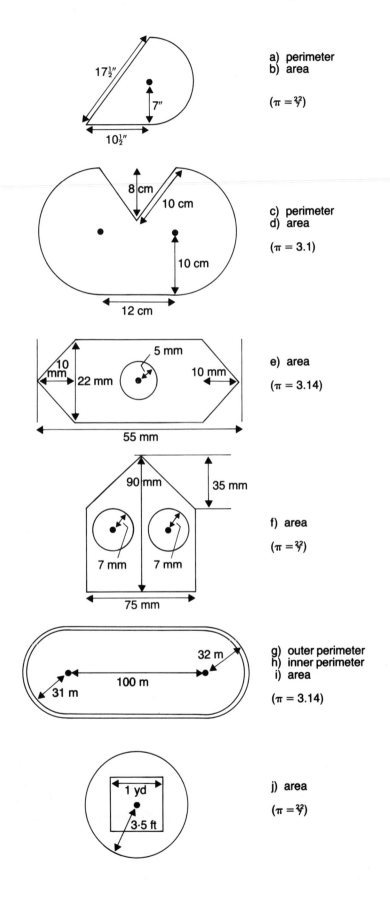

a) perimeter
b) area

$(\pi = \tfrac{22}{7})$

c) perimeter
d) area

$(\pi = 3.1)$

e) area

$(\pi = 3.14)$

f) area

$(\pi = \tfrac{22}{7})$

g) outer perimeter
h) inner perimeter
i) area

$(\pi = 3.14)$

j) area

$(\pi = \tfrac{22}{7})$

Volume and Capacity

Volume

The *volume* of an object is the amount of space the object takes up. The amount of space is measured in units based on cubes. For instance, a cubic centimetre is the space taken up by a cube with sides 1 cm.

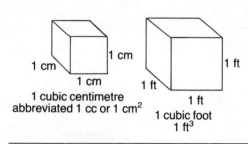

1 cubic centimetre
abbreviated 1 cc or 1 cm^2

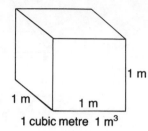

1 cubic foot
1 ft^3

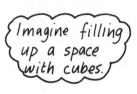

1 cubic metre 1 m^3

Imagine filling up a space with cubes.

Cuboids

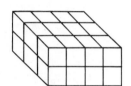

A rectangular box is called a *cuboid*. A cuboid can be divided into a number of unit cubes. Its volume is this number of unit cubes.

Volume = number of unit cubes

You can see from the diagram that the volume of a cuboid, or rectangular box is:

$$length \times height \times width$$

The length, height and width must be in the same units.

This can be written as the formula: $V = l \times h \times w$

Examples:

■ What is the volume of a box which is 2 m by 3 m by 4 m?

→ $2 \times 3 \times 4 = 24$ → volume 24 m^3

■ What is the volume of a box which is 5 cm by 36 mm by 4 cm?

→ change the 36 mm into centimetres = $36 \div 10 = 36$ cm
→ = $5 \times 3.6 \times 4 = 72$
→ volume = 72 cm^3
Answer: volume = 72 cm^3

■ What is the volume of a cube of side 6 m?

Each side of a cube is the same length.

so $l = 6$ $h = 6$ and $w = 6$
$V = 6 \times 6 \times 6 = 216$

Answer: volume = 216 m^3

Practice 1

Calculate the volumes of these rectangular boxes:
a) 4 cm by 3 cm by 2 cm
b) 25 mm by 2 cm by 10 mm
c) 1 m by 90 cm by 0.5 m
d) 852 mm by 2 m by 50 cm
e) 50 cm cube
f) A central heating oil tank is 2 ft wide, 4 ft high and 4 ft long. What is its volume?

Other shapes

Imagine a cube of plasticene with sides 1 cm. This cube has volume 1 cm³. You can change the plasticene into many different shapes. Each of these different shapes has volume 1 cm³. So you can see that shapes other than cubes and cuboids can have volumes given in cubic units.

Capacity

The *capacity* of a container is how much it will hold. The capacity of a milk bottle is 1 pint. It will hold 1 pint of milk. The capacity of a car's petrol tank is 50 litres (Austin Maestro).

The metric measures of capacity are based on the litre. A space of 1000 cubic centimetres will hold 1 litre. The litre is divided into 1000 smaller units called millilitres. You often see the 'size' of a product given in millilitres on the label. Look at the toothpaste and shampoo in your bathroom. Centilitres (a hundredth of litre) are also used.

You need to remember
100 centilitres (cl) = 1 litre
1000 millilitres (ml) = 1 litre

1 litre = 1000 cm³
1 litre = 1000 ml   So 1 ml = 1 cm³

The 'old fashioned' imperial units of capacity are still used quite commonly. I've already mentioned the pint, used for milk and beer among other things. The gallon is still used for petrol, but litres are trying to take over!

You need to remember
8 pints = 1 gallon (gal)

Examples:

■ Express 255 cl in litres.

100 cl = 1 l
255 ÷ 100 = 2.55
∴ 255 cl = 2.55 l

63

■ Write in order of size, smallest first: 40 cl, 8 ml, 5 l.

Convert into the same units, ml will do.
40 cl = 40 × 10 ml = 400 ml
5 l = 5 × 1000 ml = 5000 ml
In order of size: 8 ml, 400 ml, 5000 ml.
That is: 8 ml, 40 cl, 5 l.

■ A tank has internal measurements 1 m × 40 cm × 50 cm.
What is its capacity in litres?

1 cm³ = 1 ml.
Convert all dimensions to centimetres. Well, there's only
1 m to convert!
Volume of tank = 100 × 40 × 50 = 200 000 cm³
Capacity of tank = 200 000 ml
1 litre = 1 000 ml
200 000 ÷ 1000 = 200
Capacity of tank = 200 litres.

Practice 2

Copy and complete:

a) 360 cl = ... litres
b) 0.75 l = ... cl.
c) 450 ml = ... l.
d) 5.263 l = ... ml.
e) 15 cl = ... ml.
f) 56 ml = ... cl.
g) 36 pints = ... gallons
h) $7\frac{1}{4}$ gals = ... pints

Practice 3

a) Put these capacities in order of size, smallest first:
   0.78 litres   2400 ml   175 cl
b) Put these capacities in order of size, smallest first:
   2.5 litres   220 cl   2400 ml
c) Calculate the capacity, in litres, of a petrol can which
   has the following dimensions:
   40 cm by 13 cm by 12 cm.
d) How much water is there in a bath which is 1.6 m long
   and 54 cm wide? The water is 300 mm deep. Imagine
   the bath is rectangular.
   Give your answer in litres.

Metric and Imperial Conversions

As both the metric and imperial systems of measurement are commonly used in Britain today, it's important to be able to switch easily from one system to the other.

Many products have labels showing the quantities in both metric and imperial units.

Examples:

■ A bar of soap is labelled 3 oz and 87 g. Approximately how many grams are there in 1 ounce?

$$3 \text{ ounces} = 87 \text{ gram}$$
$$\therefore 1 \text{ ounce} = 87 \div 3 = 29 \text{ g}$$
There are 29 grams in an ounce.

(This is approximate because the weights on the packet would have been approximate.)

■ A can of cola is labelled 300ml and 11.6 fluid ounces (fl oz). How many millilitres are there in 1 fluid ounce?

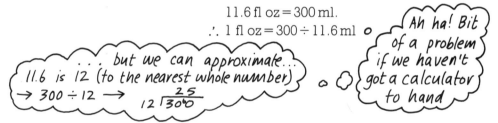

$$11.6 \text{ fl oz} = 300 \text{ ml.}$$
$$\therefore 1 \text{ fl oz} = 300 \div 11.6 \text{ ml}$$

... but we can approximate...
11.6 is 12 (to the nearest whole number)
→ 300 ÷ 12 → $12\overline{)300}$ $\frac{25}{}$

Ah ha! Bit of a problem if we haven't got a calculator to hand

There are about 25 ml in 1 fl oz.

Practice 1

The following table shows a number of products and their size in both metric and imperial units. In the last column work out the approximate conversion required.

	Product	Metric size	Imperial size	Conversion required
a)	Spice	100 g	3.5 oz	1 g = ... ounces
b)	Men's trousers	76 cm	30 inches	1 inch = ... cm
c)	Mushroom gravy	50 ml	2 fl oz	1 fl oz = ... ml
d)	Yoghurt juice	200 ml	7 fl oz	1 fl oz = ... ml
e)	Vinegar	284 ml	$\frac{1}{2}$ pint	1 pint = ... ml
f)	Cling film	30 m	33 yards	1 m = ... yards
g)	Baked beans	447 g	$15\frac{3}{4}$ oz	1 lb = ... grams
h)	Aluminium foil	4.5 m	15 ft	1m = ... ft
i)	Salad cream	285 g	10.1 oz	1 oz = ... grams
j)	Miniwheats	500 g	1.1 lb	1 kg = ... lbs

Conversions

You don't need to learn the conversions from metric to imperial units, you can generally look them up (and they'll be given to you in arithmetic tests). Here are a few of the important ones:

Length
8 km = 5 miles
1 m = 39 inches
1 inch = 2.54 cm

Warning! All these conversions are approximate.

Mass or Weight
1 kg = 2.2 lbs
1 lb = 454 g
1 oz = 28 g

Capacity
1 litre = 1.76 pints = $1\frac{3}{4}$ pints
1 pint = 568 ml

Examples:

■ It is 312 km from Calais to Paris. How far is this in miles?

$$8 \text{ km} = 5 \text{ miles}$$
$$\therefore 1 \text{ km} = \frac{5}{8} \text{ mile}$$
$$\therefore 312 \text{ km} = 312 \times \frac{5}{8} \text{ mile}$$
$$312 \text{ km} = 195 \text{ miles}$$

■ A recipe requires 4 oz of sugar. How much is this in grams?

$$1 \text{ oz} = 28 \text{ g}$$
$$\therefore 4 \text{ oz} = 4 \times 28 = 112 \text{ g}$$
$$4 \text{ oz} = 112 \text{ g}$$

Practice 2

Make the following conversions:
a) 8 inches into cm
b) 5 kg into pounds
c) $1\frac{1}{2}$ lb into grams
d) $\frac{1}{2}$ litre into pints
e) 200 miles into kilometres
f) 423 km into miles
g) 1 foot into millimetres
h) 5 lb into kg
i) 1 gallon into litres
j) 1 yd. into cm

Conversion tables

Example:

Tables and graphs are often produced to make conversions quick and easy. Here is an example:

■ Petrol price is often now given in pence per litre. You sometimes find a table, like this, to convert the price into pence per gallon at the filling station.

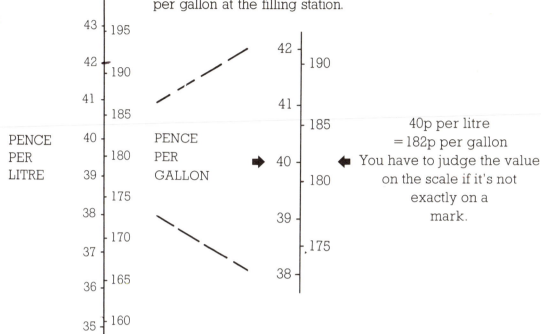

40p per litre
= 182p per gallon
You have to judge the value on the scale if it's not exactly on a mark.

Practice 3

Using the conversion table, convert these prices:
a) 42p per litre
b) 177p per gallon
c) £2 per gallon
d) 39.5p per litre
e) 35.2p per litre

Temperature

Temperature is measured in two units, degrees Fahrenheit (°F) and degrees Celsius (°C). You can convert from Celsius to Fahrenheit, but *it must be done in a special way*. Here is a diagram to show how it is done:

°Celsius → Multiply by 9 → Divide by 5 ⟶ Add 32 → °Fahrenheit

°Fahrenheit → Subtract 32 → Multiply by 5 → Divide by 9 → °Celsius

---

Practice 4

Convert the following temperatures:

to °C	to °F
a) 10°C	f) 50°F
b) 20°C	g) 62°F
c) 15°C	h) 83°F
d) 4°C	i) 20°F
e) 18°C	j) 8°F

Longer Problems(B)

1. A can contains 5 litres of motor oil.
   a) The oil is priced at £7.15 per can. How much is this per litre?
   b) Convert 5 litres into cubic centimetres.
   c) In an oil change a car requires 4.25 litres. How much oil would be left in the can if a full one was used for the oil change?
   d) The manufacturers launch a promotion in which 10% extra is given away free. How much oil will a can hold during the promotion?
   e) The can measures 17 cm by 11 cm by 34 cm. What is the volume of the can?

2. Sheets of computer paper measure 11 in by 21 mm. A curious size, being a mix of metric and imperial units.
   a) 1 inch $\simeq$ 25.4 mm
   b) Calculate 25.4×10.
   Calculate 25.4×9.
   Write down the length 241 mm in inches, correct to the nearest inch.
   c) Given that the paper size is approximately 0.28 m by 0.24 m, calculate the area of one sheet of paper.
   d) The paper weighs 60 grams per square metre. The box contains 2000 sheets. What is the weight of paper in the box? Give your answer in kilograms.

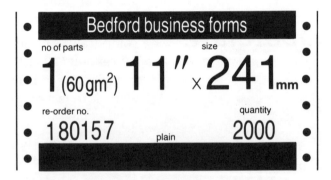

3. A standard print size for a photograph is 5 in × 3½ in.
   a) What is the area of the photograph.

   A company advertises that it provides 30% bigger prints.
   b) What is 30% of the area you calculated for part (a)?
   c) What would be the area of a print that was 30% bigger than the standard print?
   d) This company provides prints which are 6 in × 4 in, instead of the standard size. Is it true that they offer 30% bigger prints than the standard size?
   e) 20 prints cost £2.05. What is the cost per print to the nearest penny?

4 To convert from a temperature in degrees Celsius to degrees Fahrenheit, you multiply by 9, then divide by 5 and add 32.
  a) Convert 4°C to °F.
  b) Write this answer to one significant figure.

  The wind chill chart, below, shows the temperature experienced by a person when there is a wind. The experienced reduction in temperature from that shown on a thermometer is called '*wind chill*'.
  c) When the actual thermometer reading is 40°F and the wind speed is 30 mph, what temperature will a mountaineer experience?
  d) In this case, what is the drop in temperature due to wind chill.

WIND CHILL CHART

As wind has an important effect on the temperature it is most advisable to use a tent or bivouac shelter when sleeping in cold weather or at high altitude in windy weather.

ESTIMATED WIND SPEED IN MPH	ACTUAL THERMOMETER READING (°F)											
	50	40	30	20	10	0	−10	−20	−30	−40	−50	−60
	EQUIVALENT TEMPERATURE (°F)											
calm	50	40	30	20	10	0	−10	−20	−30	−40	−50	−60
5	48	37	27	16	6	−5	−15	−26	−36	−47	−57	−68
10	40	28	16	4	−9	−21	−33	−46	−58	−70	−83	−95
15	36	22	9	−5	−18	−36	−45	−58	−72	−85	−99	−112
20	32	18	4	−10	−25	−39	−53	−67	−82	−96	−110	−124
25	30	16	0	−15	−29	−44	−59	−74	−88	−104	−118	−133
30	28	13	−2	−18	−33	−48	−63	−79	−94	−109	−125	−140
35	27	11	−4	−20	−35	−49	−67	−82	−98	−113	−129	−145
40	26	10	−6	−21	−37	−53	−69	−85	−100	−116	−132	−148

(wind speeds greater than 40 mph have little additional effect)	LITTLE DANGER (for properly clothed person)	INCREASING DANGER	GREAT DANGER
			Danger from freezing of exposed flesh

IMPORTANT! ALWAYS KEEP THIS CHART HANDY. DON'T BE CAUGHT OUT

5 Some hire charges for car tools from an equipment hire company are set out below.
  a) A DIY car repairer hires a Car Body Sander and a Panel Beating Kit for a day. How much will this cost?
  b) Another DIY enthusiast hires a Battery Charger for 3 days. How much will this cost?
  c) A 10% discount from the day rate is offered for hires of eight hours or less. What will it cost to hire a socket set for six hours?
  d) These prices *exclude* VAT. This is charged at 15%. What would it cost to hire a Panel Beating Kit for a week including VAT?

car tools

	first 24 hrs	extra days	week
battery charger	3·50	1·40	7·00
car body sander	5·00	2·00	10·00
panel beating kit	4·50	1·80	9·00
socket set	3·00	1·20	6·00

Time and Timetables

Time can be given in two main ways, using a twelve hour clock or a twenty-four hour clock.

A twelve hour clock is commonly used in everyday speech. It's what appears on most watches and times of events are advertised in this way.

The twenty-four hour clock is used in official circumstances. You find it on timetables and so it is very important to understand it well.

Using the twelve hour clock

The way that you say a time and the way you write it down are often different. For instance, 'quarter to three' is usually written 2.45 and that's what a digital watch will show. The diagrams show some of these differences:

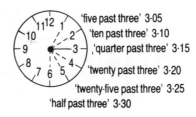

'five past three' 3·05
'ten past three' 3·10
'quarter past three' 3·15
'twenty past three' 3·20
'twenty-five past three' 3·25
'half past three' 3·30

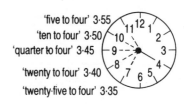

'five to four' 3·55
'ten to four' 3·50
'quarter to four' 3·45
'twenty to four' 3·40
'twenty-five to four' 3·35

Each day there are two twelve hour cycles. The period that starts at midnight and goes on to midday is called am and the one that follows, midday until midnight is pm.

So 3am is three in the morning, 3pm is three in the afternoon.

Lengths of time

You need to remember
60 seconds = 1 minute
60 minutes = 1 hour
24 hours = 1 day

You need to be able to find how long something lasts, for example a journey or TV programme.

Example:

■ A country walk takes someone from 9.35 until 11.25. This walk takes:

9.35→10.35 → 10.45 → 10.55 → 11.05 → 11.15 → 11.25
1 hour   10 mins   10 mins   10 mins   10 mins   10 mins

1 hour 50 mins

(It is not very wise to try a subtraction sum. It is better to count on in time as in this example.)

Practice 1

The diagram shows a summary of BBC television programmes for 20/12/86. What was the length of the following programmes?

BBC1 ▮▮ TODAY AT A GLANCE ▮▮ BBC2

8.30	The Family-Ness		
8.35	The Muppet Babies		
9.0	Saturday SuperStore	9.0	Pages from Ceefax
		11.0	Carols for Christmas
		11.50	2001: A Space Odyssey
12.15	Grandstand		
	Note; 2.5 means 2.05.	2.5	Harold Lloyd's World of Comedy
		3.40	Anna Neagle in Piccadilly Incident
5.5	News, Weather, Sport		
5.20	Bob's Full House	5.20	Sounds of Christmas
5.55	Oliver!		
		6.10	International Bridge Club
		6.40	Cameo
		6.50	NewsView
		7.30	Oberon
8.15	The Paul Daniels Magic Show		
9.0	Casualty		
9.50	News, Sport, Weather	9.50	All Passion Spent
10.5	Sir Harry – A Celebration		
11.15	Tarzan, the Ape Man	10.45-1.20	The Film Club: The Wages of Fear
1.5-1.10	Weather		

a) *Saturday SuperStore*
b) *The Muppet Babies*
c) *Oliver!*
d) All the news programmes
e) BBC1's broadcasts that day
f) You decide to record *2001: A Space Odyssey* and *Tarzan, the Ape Man* to watch later. Will these films both fit on the same 3 hour video tape?
g) A cake is put in the oven at a quarter past three. It takes 50 minutes to bake. At what time will it be ready?

Twenty-four hour clock

Twenty-four hour clock times are easy to recognise. They all have four figures, eg 17.45, and they don't use am or pm.

Converting from the twelve hour clock is simple for times before midday.

Examples:

■ 3 am = 03.00 (Note the added zero, just 3.00 would be wrong.)
■ 2.30 am = 02.30   ■ 11.55 am = 11.55

At midday the twenty-four hour clock carries on counting the hours: 13, 14, 15, . . .

Examples:

■ 2 pm = 14.00   ■ 5.30 pm = 17.30   ■ 10.35 pm = 22.35

Practice 2

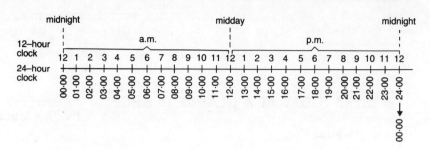

a) Convert these times to the twenty-four hour clock:
   3.30 am, 8.30 pm, 1.55 pm, 10.47 am, 10.47 pm

b) Convert these times to the twelve hour clock.
   Remember to say whether the time is am or pm.
   03.45, 12.50, 18.20, 21.37, 00.05

c) What time would you have set the video (twenty-four
   hour clock) to record these programmes. Remember to
   give the starting and finishing times. *2001: A Space
   Odyssey, Tarzan, the Ape Man*

d) Using the twenty-four hour clock, write down the time
   seventeen minutes after:
   13.35, 11.53, 09.43, 23.50, 23.43

e) It is 13.45 in London and 08.45 in New York. What is the
   time difference between these two cities?

Timetables

Timetables always use the twenty-four hour clock. They
often look extremely daunting, but with a bit of practice
they can be easily understood.

On the opposite page is the rail timetable between
Sittingbourne and Sheerness-on-Sea.

Examples:

■ A woman wants to travel from Sittingbourne to Sheerness.
The earliest she can get to the station is half past three.

This is 15.30 in the twenty-four hour clock. Looking at the
timetable you can see that the train she should catch is the
15.49 which arrives in Sheerness at 16.06. This journey
takes 17 minutes.

■ What is the latest you can catch a train from Sittingbourne
to Swale?

This is the 19.52 from Sittingbourne. No train stops at
Swale after 20.00.

■ I want to get from Kemsley to Queenborough by a quarter
to two.

This is 13.45, that's between 08.32 and 15.32 when
trains run hourly. So the train to catch is the one which
arrives at 13.32, and this departs Kemsley at 13.23.

Rather than list every possible train you are told that the same minutes past each hour apply between 0800 and 1500.

24 hour clock in use. Time written without a point. (i.e. 0655 = 06.55)

Different timetables often apply for Saturday and Sunday.

Table 213

Mondays to Fridays

Sittingbourne — Sheerness-on-Sea

Miles		MX 2	2 A		2	2		2	2			2	2				2		2		2		2			2
0	**Sittingbourne..212 d**	0020	0545	....	0613	0631	....	0655	0715	....	....	0735	0750	....	....	....	0819		1519	....	1549	....	1619	....	....	1649
2	Kemsley ....d	0024	0549	..	0617	0635	..	0659	0719	..	..	0739	0754	..	..	..	0823	and	1523	..	1553	..	1623	..	..	1653
4	Swale ....d	....	0553	....	0621	0639	....	0703	0723	....	....	0743	0758	....	....	....	0827	every	1527	....	1557	....	1627	....	....	1657
6	Queenborough.........d	0032	0558	..	0629b	0650c	..	0712e	0730	..	..	0750	0805	..	..	..	0832	hour until	1532	..	1602	..	1632	..	..	1702
8	**Sheerness-on-Sea a**	0036	0602	....	0633	0654	....	0716	0734	....	....	0754	0809	....	....	....	0836		1536	....	1606	....	1636	....	....	1706

	2			2		2			2	C			2		2			2	2			2		2			
Sittingbourne ...212 d	1719	....	....	1756	....	1821	....	....	1844	....	....	....	1924	....	1952	....	....	2020	2120	....	....	2220	....	2320	....	....	....
Kemsley ....d	1723	..	..	1800	..	1825	..	..	1848	1901	..	..	1928	..	1956	..	..	2024	2124	..	..	2224	..	2324	..	..	..
Swale ....d	1727	....	....	1804	....	1829	....	....	1853	1905	....	....	1932	....	2000	....	....	....	....	....	....	....	....	....	....	....	....
Queenborough ....d	1732	..	..	1809	..	1834	..	..	1858	1910	..	..	1937	..	2005	..	..	2032	2133	..	..	2232	..	2332	..	..	..
Sheerness-on-Sea...a	1736	....	....	1813	....	1838	....	....	1902	1914	....	....	1941	....	2009	....	....	2036	2137	....	....	2236	....	2336	....	....	....

d indicates time of departure of train from station
a indicates time of arrival.

. . . means the train does not stop at this station

Practice 3

Here's the train timetable between London and Ashford.

Table 198

Mondays to Fridays

London → Maidstone East and Ashford (Kent).

Miles	Miles		MX	MX	A	C	D	E														
0	0	**London Victoria** ⊖ 195, 212 d	....	....	0550	0620	0650	0720	0753	0827	....	0857	0927	0957	1027	1057	1127	1157	1227	....	1257	1327
—	4¼	Denmark Hill 176, 195, 201 d	..	..	..	..	..	..	..	..	..	..	..	..	..	1106	..	1206	..	..	1306	..
—	5	Peckham Rye 176, 178, 179, 195, 201 d	....	....	....	....	....	....	....	....	....	....	....	....	....	1108	....	1208	....	....	1308	....
11	—	Bromley South 195, 212 d	..	..	0606	0636	0706	0736	0814	0843	..	0919	0943	1016	1043	1119	1143	1219	1243	..	1319	1343
14¾	—	St. Mary Cray 195, 212 d	....	....	0612	0642	0712	0743	0820	....	....	0925	....	1022	....	1125	....	1225	....	....	1325	....
17½	—	Swanley 195, 212 d	..	..	0617	0647	0717	0748	0825	..	..	0929	..	1027	..	1130	..	1230	..	..	1330	..
24	—	Otford 195 d	....	0006	0626	0656	0726	0757	0834	....	....	0939	....	1036	....	1139	....	1239	....	....	1339	....
27	—	Kemsing d	..	..	..	0701	0731	0802	0839	..	..	0943	..	1041	..	1144	..	1244	..	..	1344	..
29½	—	Borough Green & Wrotham d	....	0014	0634	0705	0735	0806	0843	0907	....	0948	1007	1046	1107	1149	1207	1249	1307	....	1349	1407
34¾	—	West Malling d	..	0020	0640	0712	0742	0813	0850	..	..	0954	..	1052	..	1155	..	1255	..	..	1355	..
35¾	—	East Malling d	....	0023	....	0714	0744	0815	0852	....	....	0957	....	1055	....	1158	....	1258	....	....	1358	....
37½	—	Barming d	0001	0026	..	0718	0748	0819	0856	..	..	1001	..	1058	..	1201	..	1301	..	..	1401	..
40	—	**Maidstone East** a	0006	0031	0648	0722	0752	0823	0900	0920	....	1006	1020	1103	1120	1206	1220	1306	1320	....	1406	1420
—	—	d	0007	0033	0650	0724	0754	0824	0907	0922	..	1007	1022	1107	1122	1207	1222	1307	1322	..	1407	1422
42¾	—	Bearsted d	0012	0038	0655	0729	0759	0829	0912	0927	....	1012	1027	1112	1127	1212	1227	1312	1327	....	1412	1427
45	—	Hollingbourne d	0016	0042	0659	0733	0803	0833	..	0931	..	..	1031	..	1131	..	1231	..	1331	..	..	1431
47½	—	Harrietsham d	0020	0046	0703	0737	0807	0837	....	0935	....	....	1035	....	1135	....	1235	....	1335	....	....	1435
49¼	—	Lenham d	0023	0049	0706	0740	0810	0840	0920	0938	..	1020	1038	1120	1138	1220	1238	1320	1338	..	1420	1438
53¼	—	Charing d	0028	0054	0711	0745	0815	0845	....	0943	....	....	1043	....	1143	....	1243	....	1343	....	....	1443
59¼	—	**Ashford (Kent)** 207 a	0036	0102	0719	0753	0823	0853	0932	0951	..	1032	1051	1132	1151	1232	1251	1332	1351	..	1432	1451

			G		J					K	L		N									
London Victoria ⊖ 195, 212 d	1357	1427	1457	1527	1603	1638	....	1658	1717	1737	....	1758	1830	1857	1927	....	1957	2057	2157	2257	2327	....
Denmark Hill 176, 195, 201 d	1406	..	1506	..	..	..	..	..	..	..	..	..	..	..	..	..	2006	2106	2206	2306	..	..
Peckham Rye 176, 178, 179, 195, 201 d	1408	....	1508	....	....	....	....	....	....	....	....	....	....	....	....	....	2008	2108	2208	2308	....	....
Bromley South 195, 212 d	1419	1443	1519	1543	1623	1654	..	1714	1733	1754	1807	1814	1849	1916	1943	..	2019	2119	2219	2319	2343	..
St. Mary Cray 195, 212 d	1425	....	1525	....	1629	1700	....	....	1739	....	1813	1820	1855	1922	....	....	2025	2125	2225	2325	2349	....
Swanley 195, 212 d	1430	..	1530	..	1633	1705	..	1723	1744	..	1818	1825	1900	1927	..	..	2030	2130	2230	2330	2354	..
Otford 195 d	1439	....	1539	....	1643	1714	....	1732	1753	1811	1829	1835	1909	1936	2000	....	2039	2139	2239	2339	0006	....
Kemsing d	1444	..	1544	..	1647	1719	..	..	1758	..	1834	1840	..	1941	..	..	2044	2144	2244	2344	..	..
Borough Green & Wrotham d	1449	1507	1549	1607	1652	1724	....	1740	1803	1819	1838	1844	1917	1945	2008	....	2049	2149	2249	2349	0014	....
West Malling d	1455	..	1555	..	1658	1730	..	1747	1809	1825	1845	1851	1923	1952	2014	..	2055	2155	2255	2355	0020	..
East Malling d	1458	....	1558	....	1701	....	....	1749	1812	....	1847	1853	1926	1954	....	....	2058	2158	2258	2358	0023	....
Barming d	1501	..	1601	..	1704	1735	..	1752	1815	..	1851	1857	1929	1958	..	..	2101	2201	2301	0001	0026	..
Maidstone East a	1506	1520	1606	1620	1709	1740	....	1757	1819	1833	1855	1901	1934	2002	2022	....	2106	2206	2306	0006	0031	....
d	1507	1522	1607	1622	1710	1742	..	1758	1820	1833	1856	1902	1934	..	2023	..	2107	2207	2308	0007	0033	..
Bearsted d	1512	1527	1612	1627	1715	1747	....	1803	1825	1838	1901	1907	1939	....	2028	....	2112	2212	2313	0012	0038	....
Hollingbourne d	..	1531	1616	1631	1719	1751	..	1807	1829	..	..	1911	1943	..	2032	..	2116	2216	2317	0016	0042	..
Harrietsham d	....	1535	1620	1635	1723	1755	....	1811	1833	1844	....	1915	1947	....	2036	....	2120	2220	2321	0020	0046	....
Lenham d	1520	1538	1623	1638	1726	1758	..	1814	1836	1847	1909	1918	1951	..	2039	..	2123	2223	2324	0023	0049	..
Charing d	....	1543	1628	1643	1731	1803	....	1819	1841	....	....	1923	1956	....	2044	....	2128	2228	2329	0028	0054	....
Ashford (Kent) 207 a	1532	1551	1636	1651	1739	1811	..	1827	1850	1859	1921	1931	2004	..	2052	..	2136	2236	2336	0036	0102	..

a) What time does the 08.57 from Victoria arrive in Ashford? How long is the journey?
b) The earliest you can reach London Victoria is 11.30 am. What time can you catch a train to Ashford?
c) The earliest you can reach London Victoria is a quarter to nine in the evening. What time can you catch a train to Ashford?
d) You arrive at Bromely South at 11 am. How long do you have to wait for the next train to Hollingbourne? What time does it arrive in Hollingbourne? How long does the journey take?
e) You arrive at Swanley station at twenty-five to ten in the morning. When is the earliest you can get to Hollingbourne directly? Can you do the journey more quickly by changing trains? How?
f) The 10.27 from London arrives at Ashford at 12.26. How many minutes late is it?

Speed

$$\text{Speed} = \frac{\text{distance travelled}}{\text{time taken}}$$

Example:

■ A journey of 123 miles takes 3 hours.

The average speed is $123 \div 3 = 41$ miles per hour (mph).

Speed generally varies throughout a journey. *Average* speed, however, assumes the speed to be *constant* during the journey.

Speed can be measured in many different units. Here are some:

	abbreviation
kilometres per hour	km/h
metres per second	ms^{-1}
feet per minute	ft/min

Any combination of distance units and time units can be used.

Copy and complete the following table:

distance	time taken	speed
123 miles	3 hours	41 mph
a) 56 km	4 hours	. . . . .
b) 404 m	4 secs	. . . . .
c) 36 feet	8 mins	. . . . .
d) 178 miles	5 hours	. . . . .
e) 42 km	$3\frac{1}{2}$ hours	. . . . .

f) A train leaves London Paddington at 17.25 and arrives in Bristol at 18.55. This journey is 120 miles. What is the train's average speed?

g) It takes 3 hours to fly from Glasgow to Alicante on the Costa Blanca. The distance is 1314 miles. What is the aircraft's average speed?

h) Manchester to Lisbon is 1166 miles. What is the average speed of an aircraft which takes 2 hours 45 minutes?

Journey distance

Distance travelled = average speed × time taken

$$\text{Time taken} = \frac{\text{distance travelled}}{\text{average speed}}$$

A diagram to help you choose the right formula. Cover the thing you want to work out.

Example:

■ On a long journey a driver knows she can average 40 mph. If she sets off at 9.00 am, what time will she arrive at her destination 170 miles away?

time taken = $170 \div 40 \rightarrow \frac{170}{40} = \frac{17}{4} = 4\frac{1}{4} \rightarrow$ time taken 4 hours 15 min

$\rightarrow$9–10–11–12–1$\rightarrow$arrival time 13.15 (twenty-four hour clock) or 1.15 pm

$\underbrace{\qquad\qquad}_{\text{4 hours}}$

The table shows the distance between some towns in Britain.

	Birmingham	Edinburgh	Glasgow	Leeds	London	Manchester	Newcastle
293							
291	45						
115	206	215					
117	405	402	196				
88	218	214	43	199			
198	109	150	91	280	141		

For the average speeds given, calculate the time the
following journeys would take and the estimated time of
arrival given the departure time:
a) Birmingham to Newcastle at 60 mph, departure 8 am.
b) Glasgow to Leeds at 50 mph, departure 10.30 am.
c) Manchester to Birmingham at 30 mph, departure 11.20.
d) London to Edinburgh at 45 mph, departure 6.30pm.
e) Manchester to Newcastle at 30 mph, departure 20.15.

Conversions

It is quite easy to convert from miles per hour to
kilometres per hour and vice versa because all you have
to do is convert the distances, miles to kilometres.

$$5 \text{ miles} \simeq 8 \text{ kilometres}$$

$$1 \text{ mile} \simeq \tfrac{8}{5} \text{ km} \qquad \tfrac{5}{8} \simeq 1 \text{ km}$$

$$1 \text{ mph} \simeq \tfrac{8}{5} \text{ km/h} \qquad \tfrac{5}{8} \text{ mph} \simeq 1 \text{ km/h}$$

Example:

■ $50 \text{ mph} = 50 \times \tfrac{8}{5} = 80 \text{ km/h}$

The graph shows the conversion between mph and feet
per second:
You can see that 30mph $\simeq$ 44 ft/sec.

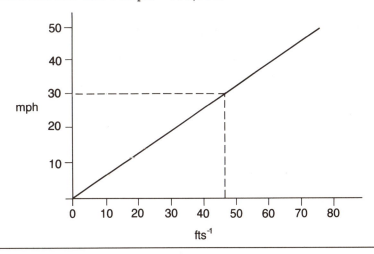

Practice 3

a) Convert the following common British speed limits
   (in mph) to km/h: 30, 40, 50, 60, 70
b) These speed limit signs were seen in France and Spain.
   Convert them to speed limits for a British motorist:

c) Using the graph above, convert the following:
   10 mph into ft/sec, 20 ft/sec into mph, 50 mph into ft/sec

Average

An *average* is a representative. It is sometimes helpful to give a single number to represent a group of numbers (set of data). For instance, it is probably more useful to know that the average 'gate' at a football ground is 9800 spectators, rather than the crowd sizes for each match in a season. The most common average to be used is the *mean average*.

Mean average

$$\text{Mean average} = \frac{\text{Sum of numbers}}{\text{Number of numbers}}$$

Example:

■ The mean average of 5, 18, 10, 8, and 11 is:

There are five numbers here.

$$\frac{5+18+10+8+11}{5} = \frac{52}{5} = 10.4$$

Practice 1

Find the mean average of these sets of numbers:
a) 7, 1, 1, 3
b) 6, 2, 2, 5, 4, 5
c) 9, 0, 2, 2, 2
d) 8, 7, 3, 3
e) 8, 1, 4, 4, 1, 2
f) The 'gates' at the last five home matches of City were 8979, 6253, 8052, 5691, and 8298. What is the average crowd size?
g) The workers at a small company get the following weekly wages: two earn £90; four earn £120; three earn £150 and the boss earns £400. What is the average weekly wage?
   Is this value a good representative figure for the weekly wage at the company?
h) Each day in June the highest temperature at a resort was recorded. The results were: 22°, 23°, 17°, 16°, 16°, 18°, 17°, 16°, 20°, 23°, 27°, 26°, 27°, 25°, 13°, 15°, 20°, 20°, 20°, 18°, 23°, 24°, 21°, 25°, 28°, 26°, 26°, 25°, 24°, 28° (all Celsius). What was the average daily maximum temperature?
i) The average height of a 15 year old boy is 1633 mm. If you laid a hundred 15 year old boys end to end how far would you expect them to stretch?

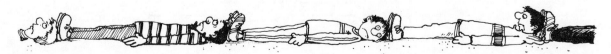

Example:

■ Find the average of 1, 5, 4 and 2.
Now find the average of 101, 105, 104 and 102.

Average of 1, 5, 4, 2 is $\dfrac{1+5+4+2}{4}=\dfrac{12}{4}=3$

Average of 101   105   104   102
$\downarrow$ $\downarrow$ $\downarrow$ $\downarrow$
100+1   100+5   100+4   100+2 →
Average = 100 + Average of 1, 5, 4, 2 = 100 + 3 = 103

Practice 2

Find the average of 6, 0, 8, 11, 1, 4.
Now find the average of the following:
a) 56, 50, 58, 61, 51, 54
b) 1006, 1000, 1008, 1011, 1001, 1004
c) 6.6, 6.0, 6.8, 7.1, 6.1, 6.4,
d) 12, 0, 16, 22, 2, 8
e) 3, 0, 4, $5\frac{1}{2}$, $\frac{1}{2}$, 2
f) 60, 0, 80, 110, 10, 40

Ratio

Ratios compare quantities. Here are some examples:

To prepare the cocktail 'Bucks fizz' mix:

one part chilled fresh orange juice

one part chilled champagne

A mortar mixture can be made with:

one part cement
three parts sand

A bookmaker offers odds of 11–2 on a horse winning a race.

These are three examples of the use of ratio to compare two like quantities. By 'like' it is meant that the quantities are both volumes, or both lengths, or both amounts of money. Given a ratio, you use the measures you want, but both quantities must have the same units. To make a few glasses of 'Bucks fizz' you might mix 75 cl of juice with 75 cl (a bottle) champagne. A spadeful of cement mixed with 3 spadefuls of sand will make a small quantity of mortar. A £2 bet on the horse above would win £11, if it came first.

Ratios are often written using a : symbol.

orange : champagne   prize : stake
1 : 1   11 : 2
cement : sand
1 : 3

Keeping to the same ratio

The same strength mortar mix could be made with:

spadefuls cement		spadefuls sand
1	:	3
2	:	6
3	:	9
4	:	12
12	:	36

So 1 : 3   2 : 6   3 : 9   4 : 12   and 12 : 36   are all the same ratios

1   :   3   The ratio stays the same
↓ × 12   ↓ × 12   as long as you multiply both
12 : 36   sides by the same amount,
                  just like equivalent fractions.

A ratio can sometimes be simplified by the opposite process.

Examples:

■ Simplify the ratio 14 : 49:

14   :   49   The ratio stays the same
↓ ÷ 7   ↓ ÷ 7   as long as you divide both
2   :   7   sides by the same amount.

■ State the ratio of the length to the width of this carpet in its simplest form.

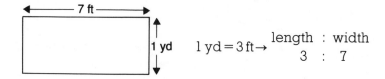

1 yd = 3 ft → length : width
                 3   :   7

■ Express $\frac{4}{3} : 7\frac{1}{3}$ as a ratio in whole numbers.

$\frac{4}{3}$: $7\frac{1}{3}$ Multiply by 3 to
               remove the fraction.
× 3↓   × 3↓
4 : 22
÷ 2↓   ÷ 2↓   Divide by 2 (common
2 : 11   factor of 4 and 22).

Practice 1

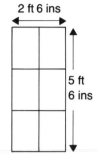

2 ft 6 ins

5 ft 6 ins

Express the following ratios in their simplest form:

a) 10 : 15
b) 10 : 15
c) 54 : 36
d) $1\frac{1}{2} : 2\frac{1}{2}$
e) $2\frac{1}{4} : 13\frac{1}{2}$

f) $2\frac{1}{3} : \frac{2}{3}$
g) height to the width of the window
h) length to the width of this page

i) How much cement should you add to 12 spadefuls of sand to make the mortar mix?
j) How much do you stand to win if you place a £5 bet on a horse at odds of 7–2?

Maps and scale

A map or plan is a bird's eye view of what's on the ground. It's a special kind of picture where all the measurements are made smaller by the same amount. This is called *scaling down*. The scale on a map or plan is often written in ratio form, for instance:

1:250 000. This means:
1 cm on the map represents 250 000 cm in real life
(or 1 mm on the map represents 250 000 mm in real life, and so on.)
Now 250 000 cm = 250 000 ÷ 100 = 2500 m
and 2500 m = 2500 ÷ 1000 = 2.5 km
1 cm represents 2.5 km

Example:

■ Two villages are 6 cm apart on a map with the scale 1.250 000. How far is this in real life?
We have seen above that the scale 1:250 000 means that 1 cm represents 2.5 km.
So 6 cm represents 6 × 2.5 = 15 km.

Practice 2

What does 1 cm represent on maps or plans with these scales?
a) 1 : 100 000
b) 1 : 25 000
c) 1 : 1000
d) 1 : 450 000

A house plan is drawn to the scale 1 : 100. What are the full scale dimensions which have these measurements on the plan?
e) living room 5 cm by 4 cm
f) kitchen 44 mm by 25 mm
g) WC 0.8 cm by 1.65 cm
h) garden 0.13 m long

Proportional parts

Here is a line which has been split in the ratio 2 : 3:

As you can see, it has been divided into a total of 5 parts.
The line is 10 cm long.
So each part is $10 \div 5 = 2$ cm.
The shorter length is 2×2 cm $= 4$ cm.
The longer length is 3×2 cm $= 6$ cm.

Example:

■ Divide 12 apples into two piles in the ratio 5 : 1.

Total number of parts $= 5 + 1 = 6$
Amount in each part $= 12 \div 6 = 2$
Larger pile $5 \times 2 = 10$
Smaller pile $1 \times 2 = 2$.

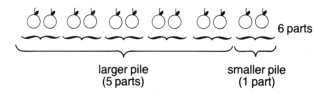

Practice 3

a) Share a dozen eggs in the ratio 2 : 1.
b) Share £21 in the ratio 3 : 4.
c) Split 50 cm in the ratio 2 : 3.
d) Divide £72 in the ratio 7 : 5.
e) Divide £1200 in the ratio 4 : 11.

Gauges and Scales

Introduction

In our everyday lives, both at home and at work, we make many measurements using a variety of gauges and scales. It is important to be able to read these scales as accurately as possible, but we must always remember that every measurement is an approximation.

■ **Example:** A measuring jug

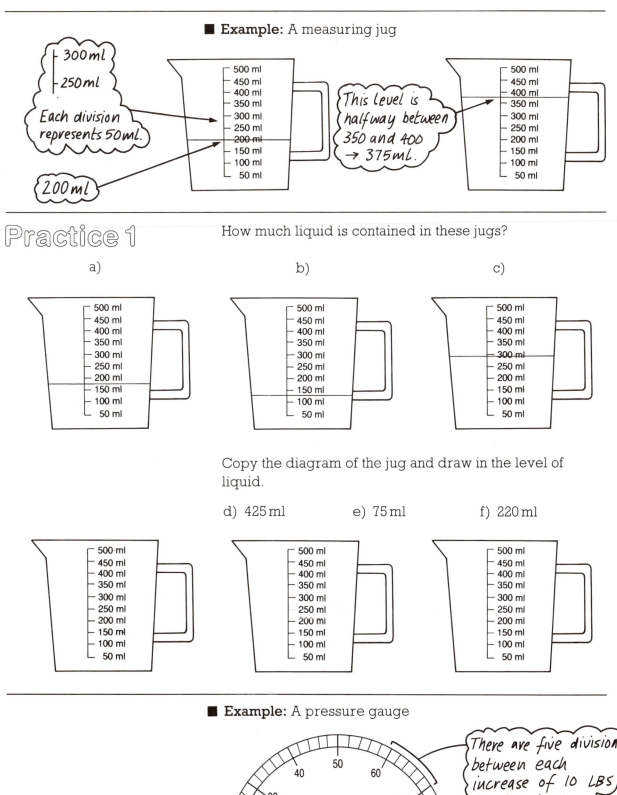

300 ml
250 ml

Each division represents 50 ml.

200 ml

This level is halfway between 350 and 400 → 375 ml.

Practice 1

How much liquid is contained in these jugs?

a)

b)

c)

Copy the diagram of the jug and draw in the level of liquid.

d) 425 ml   e) 75 ml   f) 220 ml

■ **Example:** A pressure gauge

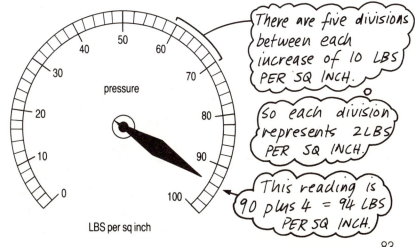

pressure

LBS per sq inch

There are five divisions between each increase of 10 LBS PER SQ INCH.

So each division represents 2 LBS PER SQ INCH.

This reading is 90 plus 4 = 94 LBS PER SQ INCH.

83

Practice 2

What is the pressure shown by these gauges?

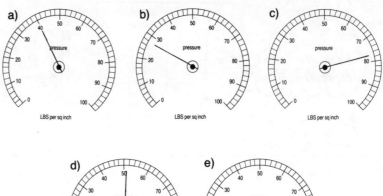

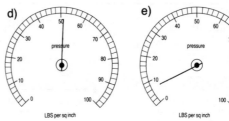

Example:

■ A car's tachometer

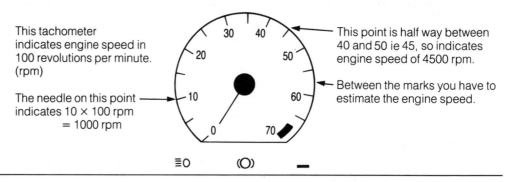

This tachometer indicates engine speed in 100 revolutions per minute. (rpm)

The needle on this point indicates 10 × 100 rpm = 1000 rpm

This point is half way between 40 and 50 ie 45, so indicates engine speed of 4500 rpm.

Between the marks you have to estimate the engine speed.

Practice 3

What is the engine speed shown by these tachometers?

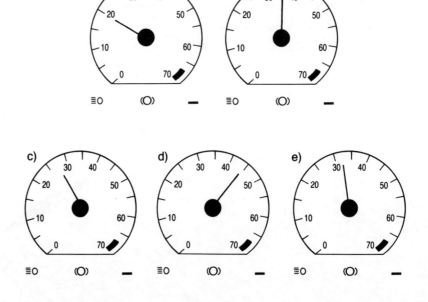

Example: A clinical thermometer

■ This thermometer reads 38°C.

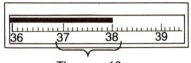

There are 10
divisions between each
degree, so each division represents
$\frac{1}{10}$ degree C or 0·1°C.

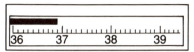

This thermometer
records 36·9°C.

Practice 4

Here are some diagrams showing clinical thermometers.
What is the temperature on each of them?

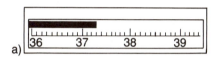

a)

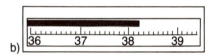

b)

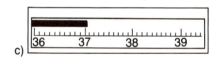

c)

Example: Household meters

■ Gas and electricity meters sometimes have dials like this:

These are from a
gas meter, measuring
cubic feet of gas.

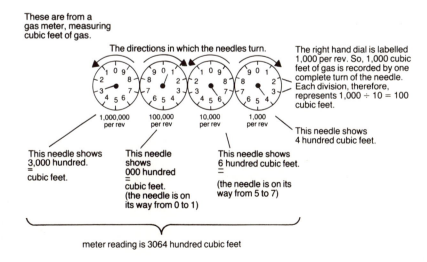

The directions in which the needles turn.

The right hand dial is labelled
1,000 per rev. So, 1,000 cubic
feet of gas is recorded by one
complete turn of the needle.
Each division, therefore,
represents 1,000 ÷ 10 = 100
cubic feet.

1,000,000
per rev
100,000
per rev
10,000
per rev
1,000
per rev

This needle shows
4 hundred cubic feet.

This needle shows
3,000 hundred.
=
cubic feet.

This needle
shows
000 hundred
=
cubic feet.
(the needle is on
its way from 0 to 1)

This needle shows
6 hundred cubic feet.
=
(the needle is on its
way from 5 to 7)

meter reading is 3064 hundred cubic feet

Read these meters:

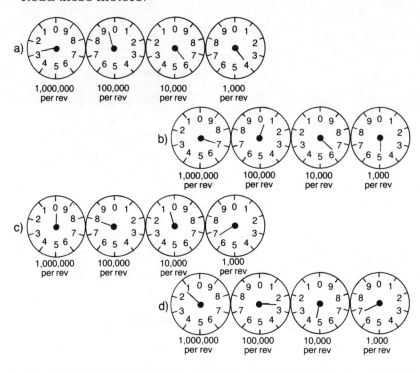

Longer Problems (C)

1   A motorist checks the milometer of his car at the beginning of a journey. It reads 29 769. At the end of the journey it reads 30 003.
   a) What is the length of the journey?
   b) The journey takes 6 hours, not counting a stop for lunch. What is the motorist's average speed?
   c) He expects to travel 35 miles on 1 gallon of petrol. What is the least whole number of gallons he used on the journey?
   d) The motorist had a $\frac{3}{4}$ hour lunch break. What time did he leave home if he arrived at his destination at 1520?

2   A room is rectangular in shape, measuring 15 ft by 12 ft. It is to be decorated.
   a) What is the perimeter of the room?
   b) The height of the ceiling above the skirting is 8 ft 11 ins. Using the table printed opposite state the number of rolls of wallpaper required to paper the room.
   c) State the dimension of the room in yards.
   d) What is the area of the ceiling in square yards?
   e) The ceiling is to be painted with *two* coats of vinyl silk paint. 1 litre is sufficient to paint 12 square yards. How much paint will be required?

HOW MUCH FINE ART WALLCOVERING YOU WILL NEED

Height from skirting	Measurement round walls including doors and windows									
Feet	28 0	32 0	36 0	40 0	44 0	48 0	52 0	56 0	60 0	64 0
7 0 to 7 6	4	4	5	5	6	6	7	7	8	8
7 7 to 8 0	4	4	5	5	6	6	7	8	8	9
8 1 to 8 6	4	5	5	6	6	7	7	8	8	9
8 7 to 9 0	4	5	5	6	6	7	8	8	9	9
9 1 to 9 6	4	5	6	6	7	7	8	9	9	10
9 7 to 10 0	5	5	6	7	7	8	9	9	10	10
10 1 to 10 6	5	5	6	7	8	8	9	10	10	11

HOW MUCH FINE ART CEILING PAPER YOU WILL NEED

Measurement in feet round room	30	40	42	50	52	60	62	66	68	72	74	78	80	84	86	88	90	94
Nº OF ROLLS	2		3		4		5		6		7		8		9		10	

All rolls 11yds long unless otherwise stated

FINE ART WALLCOVERINGS

3   A British motorist is in France and needs to buy 4 gallons of petrol.

a) Given that 1 gallon $\simeq$ 4.5 litres, how many litres should she ask for?

b) The cost of this petrol is 82 francs. The exchange rate is approximately 9.31 francs to the pound. What is the cost of this petrol, correct to the nearest pound?

c) The tyres of the car need to be pumped to a pressure of 23 pounds per sq. in. Using the conversion table below determine the pressure in kilograms per sq. cm.

Metric Tyre Pressure Conversion Chart

Pounds per sq. in	Kilograms per sq. cm	Atmospheres
14	0.98	0.95
16	1.12	1.08
18	1.26	1.22
20	1.40	1.36
22	1.54	1.49
24	1.68	1.63
26	1.83	1.76
28	1.96	1.90
30	2.10	2.04
32	2.24	2.16
36	2.52	2.44
40	2.80	2.72
50	3.50	3.40
55	3.85	3.74
60	4.20	4.08
65	4.55	4.42

4   A delicious pudding is made with the following
     ingredients:

     2 eggs
     3 oz sugar
     $1\frac{1}{2}$ oz flour
     $\frac{1}{2}$ pint milk
     $\frac{1}{4}$ pint double cream
     1 lb stoned black cherries

a) Given that 1 oz $\simeq$ 28 g, what quantity of flour is
   required in grams?
b) Given that 1 pint $\simeq$ 568 ml, how much milk is
   required in ml, correct to the nearest 100 ml?
c) What is the ratio of sugar to flour, in its simplest
   form?
d) What is the ratio of cherries to flour, in its simplest
   form?
e) The pudding takes 35 minutes to bake in the oven.
   If it is put in the oven at 11.45 am, at what time will
   it be ready?

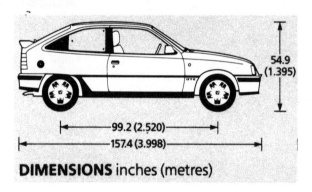

54.9
(1.395)

99.2 (2.520)
157.4 (3.998)

DIMENSIONS inches (metres)

5   The fuel consumption figures for an Astra Hatchback
     car are:

     urban driving   30.0 miles to the gallon
     at constant 56 mph   45.5 miles to the gallon
     at constant 75 mph   36.7 miles to the gallon
     (figures for automatic gearbox 1300cc model)

a) Write down the fuel consumption at constant
   75 mph correct to one significant figure.
b) An Astra is driven 270 miles around town (urban
   driving). How many gallons of petrol should the
   motorist expect the car to use?
c) On a journey of 249 miles, this car uses 7 gallons.
   What was its fuel consumption? Give your answer
   correct to one decimal place.
d) The diagram shows the length of the car in inches,
   with the length in metres in brackets. Use it to
   estimate how many inches there are in a metre,
   correct to the nearest whole unit.

6   The roof of a terraced house is to be tiled, see diagram:

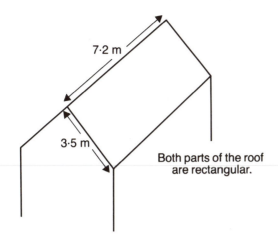

7·2 m

3·5 m

Both parts of the roof
are rectangular.

**Estimating Tables for
Plain Roof Tiles**

Sq. Metres	No. of Tiles	Sq. Metres	No. of Tiles
1	53	20	1060
2	106	30	1590
3	159	40	2120
4	212	50	2650
5	265	60	3180
6	318	70	3710
7	371	80	4240
8	424	90	4770
9	477	100	5300
10	530		

a) What is the total roof area?
b) A skylight reduces the roof area to 49 m². Using the table estimate the number of plain roof tiles to tile this roof.
c) A ridge tile is 450 mm long. How many ridge tiles will be required?

7   A price survey in five greengrocer shops finds that the price of tomatoes is 35p, 50p, 44p, 41p and 45p per pound.
a) What is the average price per pound being charged in these shops?
b) Given that 1 kg = 2.2 lb, what is the price per kilogram of the cheapest tomatoes on sale?
c) The shop charging 50p per pound decides to reduce its price to 43p. What percentage reduction is this?

8   All brands of washing powder are sold in standard size boxes. These sizes are called E3, E10, E15 and E20. The ratio of the quantity of powder in an E10 box to the quantity in an E3 box is 10 : 3. The other sizes are also in ratios given by their E number.
a) Express the ratio of powder in an E20 box to that in an E15 box in its simplest form.
b) There is 930 g of powder in an E3 box. How much powder is there in an E10 box? Give your answer in kilograms.
c) One brand costs £2.56 for an E10 box and £3.90 for an E15 box. Which is better value?
d) An E20 box costs £4.65. How much does this powder cost per kilogram?

9 A jacket is made from 35% wool, 35% polyester and the remainder is 'mixed fibre'.
   a) What is the percentage of mixed fibre?
   b) The jacket weighs 2.3 kg. What is this weight in grams?
   c) What weight of wool does the jacket contain?

10 The following electricity meter reading was taken in March.

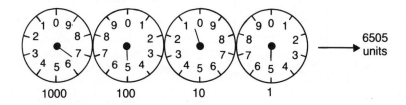

   a) In June the meter was read again. Write down the meter reading in figures.

   b) In September, the meter recorded 7832 units. On the dials below draw in the positions of the needles.

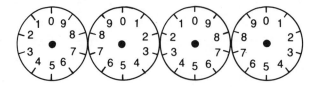

   c) How much electricity, in units, had been used between March and September?
   d) What would be the total amount charged for this electricity if the cost was 5.32p per unit?

11　The picture shows a can of cider during a promotion offering 10% free.

a) Express 10% as a fraction in its simplest form.

b) The cider company has been brewing since 1759. For how many years have they been brewers?

c) A can usually contains 440 ml. Calculate the size of a can containing exactly 10% extra.

d) The can has diameter 63 mm. Work out the circumference of the rim. (Take $\pi = \frac{22}{7}$)

12　a) A bus leaves Bristol at 06.47 and arrives in Chepstow at 07.35. How long does the journey take?

b) A person arrives at Bristol Bus Station at a quarter to three in the afternoon. Write down this time in the twenty-four hour clock.

c) Using the timetable below, write down the time of the first bus to Chepstow this person can catch.

d) Another person catches the first possible bus from Chepstow to Bristol and returns from Bristol to Chepstow on the last possible bus. How long does this person spend in Bristol?

BRISTOL·CHEPSTOW via Patchway, Severn Bridge

Service 300 via: Cheltenham Road, Horfield, Filton, Patchway, Aust Interchange, Severn Bridge.

Mondays to Fridays ⁕

BRISTOL, Bus Station	0647	0900	1010	1210	1410	1610	1745	....
Filton Church	0705	0918	1028	1228	1428	1628	1803	....
Patchway, Railway Bridge	0710	0923	1033	1233	1433	1633	1808	....
Aust Interchange	0723	0936	1046	1246	1446	1646	1821	....
CHEPSTOW, Bus Station	0735	0948	1058	1258	1458	1658	1833	....
CHEPSTOW, Bus Station	0740	0920	1010	1110	1310	1510	1710	1838
Aust Interchange	0752	0932	1022	1122	1322	1522	1722	1850
Patchway, Railway Bridge	0805	0945	1035	1135	1335	1535	1735	1903
Filton Church	0810	0950	1040	1140	1340	1540	1740	1908
BRISTOL, Bus Station	0828	1008	1058	1158	1358	1558	1758	1926

13 The map below is drawn to the scale 1 : 50 000.
   a) What length in metres is represented by 1 cm on the map?
   b) How many centimetres on the map represents 1 kilometre?
   c) It is $11\frac{1}{2}$ cm on the map from Twycross to Shackerstone. What is the actual distance, in kilometres, between these two villages?
   d) How long would it take to walk, at an average speed of 5 kmh, from Twycross to Shackerstone? Give your answer in minutes.

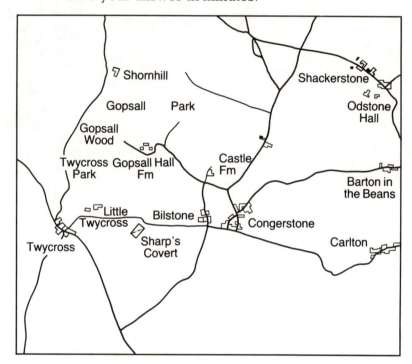

14 A worker receives £101.60 for a basic 40 hour week.
   a) How much does this worker earn in an hour?
   b) Overtime is paid at time-and-a-half, that is $1\frac{1}{2}$ times the basic hourly rate. How much does the worker earn for one hour's overtime?
   c) A worker works 45 hours one week. How much does she earn in this week?
   d) Another worker receives £109.22 in his week's paypacket. How many hours overtime did he do?

15 Pat wants to buy a home computer costing £399 excluding VAT.
   a) What is £399 to 2 significant figures?
   With some additional software the total bill is £420 plus VAT.
   b) How much VAT does Pat pay if the rate is 15%?
   c) What is the total cost including VAT?
   Pat pays a small deposit and borrows £420 at a rate of 10% simple interest over 2 years.
   d) How much will Pat pay in interest charges?
   e) What will Pat's monthly repayment be on this loan?

Answers

Place Value Practice

1 **a)** 100 **b)** 9 **c)** 8000 **d)** 600 000
5 **a)** 7.92 **b)** 6.723 **c)** 6.2007 **d)** 29.561 **e)** 5.713 **f)** 0.076 **g)** 0.7/0.70
8 1) (c) 2) (a) 3) (b) 4) (a) 5) (d) 6) (b) 7) (b) 8) (c) 9) (d) 10) (c)

Whole Numbers Practice

1 **a)** 731 **b)** 2662 **c)** 4816 **d)** 190 **e)** 10 998 **f)** 2232 **g)** 1851
  h) 836 **i)** 11 106 **j)** 1000
2 **a)** 203 **b)** 848 **c)** 116 **d)** 273 **e)** 666 **f)** 709 **g)** 63 **h)** 933 **i)** 1652
  j) 1808
3 **a)** 934 **b)** 970 **c)** 1778 **d)** 5184 **e)** 5472 **f)** 495 **g)** 9664
  h) 23 800 **i)** 18 552 **j)** 857 142
4 **a)** 74 **b)** 237 **c)** 210 **d)** 126 **e)** 475 **f)** 308 **g)** 1800 **h)** 289 **i)** 405
  j) 7003
5 **a)** 260 **b)** 1700 **c)** 46 **d)** 18 900 **e)** 70 **f)** 8600 **g)** 60 **h)** 27 600
  i) 99 000 **j)** 4800
6 **a)** 3552 **b)** 10 008 **c)** 38 924 **d)** 16 600 **e)** 27 600 **f)** 139 008
  g) 838 528 **h)** 2 285 712 **i)** 12 321 **j)** 1 234 321
7 **a)** 4, 6, 1, 0, **b)** 6, 10, 0, 10, **c)** 2, 1, 0, 0, 0
8 **a)** 10 353 **b)** 330 **c)** 40 **d)** 2450 **e)** 1500 **f)** 738 **g)** 51 miles **h)** 420

Decimals Practice

1 **a)** 7.0 **b)** 12.53 **c)** 9.33 **d)** 31 **e)** 1.012 **f)** 20.45 **g)** 26.3 **h)** 24.17
  i) 80.05 **j)** 0.073
2 **a)** 2.03 **b)** 2.76 **c)** 17.68 **d)** 44.06 **e)** 37.82 **f)** 0.467 **g)** 7.3 **h)** 9.26
  i) 0.545 **j)** 5.928
3 **a)** 15.24 **b)** 158.4 **c)** 121 **d)** 0.6104 **e)** 5.838 **f)** 76.2 **g)** 0.073
  h) 5600 **i)** 8.2 **j)** 3267
4 **a)** 15.8 **b)** 0.79 **c)** 0.1016 **d)** 2.409 **e)** 0.0708 **f)** 0.6808 **g)** 3.55
  h) 0.155 25 **i)** 0.0875 **j)** 3.875 **k)** 0.13 **l)** 0.714 285 **m)** 0.472
  n) 0.000 24 **o)** 0.0373
5 **a)** 0.75 **b)** 0.42 **c)** 0.018 **d)** 1.92 **e)** 0.02 **f)** 0.28 **g)** 6.4 **h)** 15
  i) 0.0012 **j)** 7.13
6 **a)** 0.8 **b)** 3 **c)** 2.5 **d)** 25 **e)** 20 **f)** 20 **g)** 20 **h)** 500 **i)** 62.5 **j)** 4
7 **a)** 0.7 **b)** 0.69 **c)** 711 **d)** 16.8 **e)** 6.6 **f)** 8.2 **g)** 23.6 **h)** 105.3
8 **a)** £4.47 **b)** £1.26 **c)** 26.5 miles **d)** 17.6 kg **e)** £6.30 **f)** £12.17
  g) £1.49 **h)** 1.8°

Powers, Roots, Factors and Multiples Practice

1 **a)** 81 **b)** 81 **c)** 16 **d)** 169 **e)** 64 **f)** 0.49 **g)** 0.04 **h)** 0.25 **i)** 1.44
  j) 1.21
2 **a)** 21 **b)** 80 **c)** 0 **d)** 25 **e)** 36 **f)** 32 **g)** 190 **h)** 56 **i)** 15 **j)** 22 **k)** 1
  l) 0.81 **m)** 4 **n)** 6.25 **o)** 0.06
3 **a)** 8 **b)** 10 **c)** 9 **d)** 12 **e)** 13 **f)** 25 **g)** 21 **h)** 11 **f)** 26 **j)** 30
4 **a)** 18 **b)** 36 **c)** 40 **d)** 14 **e)** 36
5 **a)** 63 **b)** 60, 64, 68 **c)** 60, 65 **d)** − **e)** 65
6 **a)** 1, 3, 5, 15 **b)** 1, 2, 3, 4, 5, 6, 10, 12, 15, 20, 30, 60 **c)** 1, 43
  d) 1, 2, 3, 4, 6, 9, 12, 18, 36 **e)** 1, 2, 5, 10, 25, 50 **f)** 1, 31
  g) 1, 2, 4, 8, 16, 32 **h)** 1, 2, 3, 5, 6, 9, 10, 15, 18, 30, 45, 90
7 **a)** 8 **b)** 7 **c)** 10 **d)** 1 **e)** 10
8 1) (b) 2) (c) 3) (a) 4) (c) 5) (c) 6) (d) 7) (d) 8) (c) 9) (a) 10) (d)

Fractions – Basic Ideas Practice

4 **a)** $\frac{12}{16}$ **b)** $\frac{6}{21}$ **c)** $\frac{5}{45}$ **d)** $\frac{14}{35}$ **e)** $\frac{14}{16}$
5 **a)** $\frac{1}{3}$ **b)** $\frac{2}{9}$ **c)** $\frac{4}{5}$ **d)** $\frac{8}{11}$ **e)** $\frac{4}{63}$ **f)** $\frac{2}{5}$ **g)** $\frac{7}{30}$ **h)** $\frac{5}{12}$ **i)** $\frac{3}{4}$ **j)** $\frac{7}{9}$
6 **a)** $\frac{2}{5}$ **b)** $\frac{5}{6}$ **c)** $\frac{3}{11}$ **d)** $\frac{4}{9}$ **e)** $\frac{3}{5}$ **f)** same **g)** $\frac{3}{8}$ **h)** $\frac{6}{7}$ **i)** $\frac{3}{14}$ **j)** $\frac{2}{7}$

Four Rules of Fractions Practice

1 a) $\frac{7}{10}$ b) $\frac{7}{8}$ c) $\frac{7}{9}$ d) $\frac{3}{4}$ e) $\frac{19}{24}$ f) $\frac{17}{35}$ g) $\frac{31}{40}$ h) $\frac{55}{63}$ i) $\frac{13}{15}$ j) $\frac{27}{28}$ k) $\frac{1}{2}$ l) $\frac{3}{8}$ m) $\frac{5}{9}$ n) $\frac{1}{4}$ o) $\frac{13}{24}$ p) $\frac{9}{35}$ q) $\frac{13}{35}$ r) $\frac{2}{9}$ s) $\frac{17}{30}$ t) $\frac{17}{36}$

2 a) $4\frac{1}{6}$ b) $5\frac{2}{3}$ c) $1\frac{8}{9}$ d) $2\frac{3}{11}$ e) 7

3 a) $\frac{13}{8}$ b) $\frac{31}{4}$ c) $\frac{27}{5}$ d) $\frac{31}{9}$ e) $\frac{33}{8}$

4 a) $1\frac{2}{3}$ b) $1\frac{1}{14}$ c) $1\frac{2}{15}$ d) $2\frac{1}{8}$ e) $1\frac{5}{18}$ f) $1\frac{11}{12}$ g) 1 h) $1\frac{13}{40}$ i) 3 j) $3\frac{1}{8}$ k) $2\frac{1}{9}$ l) $3\frac{1}{12}$ m) $3\frac{1}{10}$ n) $6\frac{1}{18}$ o) $8\frac{1}{9}$

5 a) $\frac{17}{18}$ b) $1\frac{23}{8}$ c) $1\frac{3}{16}$ d) $\frac{5}{8}$ e) $2\frac{7}{10}$ f) $\frac{5}{16}$ g) $3\frac{1}{9}$ h) $1\frac{1}{3}$ i) $4\frac{4}{15}$ j) $\frac{29}{34}$

6 a) $\frac{10}{27}$ b) $\frac{5}{36}$ c) $\frac{1}{35}$ d) $\frac{2}{9}$ e) $\frac{2}{15}$ f) $\frac{1}{4}$ g) $\frac{2}{11}$ h) $\frac{2}{21}$ i) $\frac{1}{15}$ j) $\frac{5}{14}$

7 a) 30 b) 7 c) 10 d) $12\frac{1}{2}$ e) $7\frac{1}{2}$ f) 15 g) $2\frac{1}{2}$ h) $7\frac{1}{3}$ i) $6\frac{3}{10}$ j) $15\frac{3}{4}$

8 a) $1\frac{3}{4}$ b) $\frac{1}{3}$ c) 5 d) $5\frac{3}{5}$ e) $3\frac{1}{3}$

9 a) $\frac{2}{3}$ b) $1\frac{1}{5}$ c) $3\frac{3}{4}$ d) $\frac{1}{3}$ e) $21\frac{1}{3}$ f) $4\frac{1}{2}$ g) $\frac{1}{35}$ h) $1\frac{3}{4}$ i) $\frac{1}{9}$ j) $\frac{3}{20}$

10 a) 15 b) 4 c) 10 d) 9

11 a) $\frac{2}{11}$ b) $4\frac{7}{8}$ c) $10\frac{1}{2}$ d) $1\frac{2}{5}$ e) $\frac{1}{6}$ f) $\frac{13}{60}$

Fractions and Decimals Practice

1 a) $\frac{4}{5}$ b) $\frac{9}{20}$ c) $\frac{7}{1000}$ d) $\frac{7}{200}$ e) $\frac{641}{1000}$ f) $\frac{73}{100}$ g) $\frac{13}{5000}$ h) $8\frac{1}{25}$ i) $11\frac{23}{25}$ j) $\frac{11}{20\,000}$

2 a) 0.2 b) 0.75 c) 0.375 d) 0.83 e) 0.241 f) 0.07 g) .000001 h) 0.428571 i) 0.714285 j) 0.18

3 a) 0.65 b) 0.29 c) $\frac{1}{4}$ d) 0.225 e) $\frac{5}{6}$

4 1 (c) 2 (b) 3 (b) 4 (a) 5 (a) 6 (b) 7 (b) 8 (c) 9 (a) 10 (c)

Percentages Practice

1 a) 44% b) 11%

2 a) $\frac{1}{4}$ b) $\frac{2}{5}$ c) $\frac{9}{100}$ d) $\frac{7}{20}$ e) $\frac{18}{25}$ f) $\frac{11}{25}$ g) $\frac{1}{8}$ h) $\frac{11}{200}$ i) $\frac{2}{25}$ j) $\frac{37}{40}$

3 a) 20% b) 70% c) 60% d) 25% e) 62.5% f) 35% g) 57% h) 40% i) 21.8% j) 5.5%

4 a) $\frac{1}{10}$ b) $\frac{3}{8}$ c) equal d) 90% e) $\frac{2}{3}$

5 a) 0.65, 66%, $\frac{2}{3}$ b) 9%, 0.95, $\frac{1}{10}$ c) 0.09, 10%, $\frac{1}{8}$ d) $\frac{1}{5}$, 0.219, 22% e) 49%, $\frac{1}{2}$, 0.5062

6 a) 13 ml b) 175 g c) 63 ml d) 14 tons e) 1.35 g

7 a) 240 g b) 55 m c) 288 ml d) 195 g e) 258 ml f) 180 ml g) 25% h) 500 ml i) 20 g j) 10%

Accuracy and Approximations Practice

1 a) 12 b) 5 c) 101 d) £36 e) £8 f) 1

2 a) 34 000 b) 100 c) 100 d) 260 e) 1000 f) 210 000

3 a) 360 b) 6000 c) 100 d) 3.62 e) 4.57 f) 20 g) 0.034

4 a) 6.21 b) 0.156 c) 12.8 d) 0.0

5 a) 8.57 b) 17.7 c) 540 d) 3600 e) £1.45 f) £17.51

6 a) 3.00 b) 14.2 c) 8 d) 100 e) 0 f) 2400 g) 0.004 h) 0.0 i) 1000 j) 520 000

Length and Weight Practice

1 a) 5.6 cm b) 6500 m c) 29″ d) 5.66 m e) 7040 yds f) 23 ft g) 2.566 m

2 a) 5 ft, 62 ins, 2 yds b) 1876 mm, 220 cm, 1.5 km

3 a) 61 mm, 44 mm b) 5 ins c) 38 mm d) 128 cm

4 a) 140 lb b) 2200 g c) 2.3 tonnes d) 0.23 kg e) 180 cwt f) 2240 lb

Longer Problems (A)

1 a) $\frac{1}{2}$ b) £15.15 c) £3.20
2 a) $\frac{1}{4}$ b) 24% c) $\frac{3}{20}$ d) 3 500 000 e) 525 000
3 a) 39% b) 17 000 c) 10 120 d) 27.5%
4 a) 26p b) 15p c) 30% d) £2.75
5 a) $\frac{3}{2}$ b) $\frac{2}{3}$ c) 10.64

Money Practice

2 a) £14.44, £519.84 b) 50.41, £604.94 c) £37.55, £1351.80
   d) £115.50, £2772 e) £98, £2352

More Money Practice

1 a) £1.75 b) £2.34 c) £8.82 d) £9 e) £13.68 f) £1 g) 92p h) £1.30
   i) £13.20 j) £3.85
2 a) £21.90 b) £26 c) £24 d) £4.50 e) £25 f) £9.60
3 a) £3.45 b) £5.29 c) £1.73 d) £2.71 e) £1.04 f) £95.45
   g) £163.30 h) £75.33 i) £29.27 j) £19.24
4 a) £304 b) £190 c) £5.85 d) £15.75 e) £19.80 f) £3.89
5 a) £32 b) £1180 c) £31 d) £246 e) £81 f) £1440 g) £15 h) £150
6 a) 44p b) 7.27 c) 21p d) 3p e) 10p f) £6.93 g) 6p h) 18p i) £11.80
   j) £18

Area and Perimeter Practice

1 a) 35 cm b) 52 mm c) 182 ins d) 32 m e) 312 cm
2 a) and d), b) and c)
3 a) 104 cm b) 18 ins c) 13 mm d) 18.5 cm e) 18 ins
4 a) 18.84 cm b) 44 ft c) $30\frac{4}{5}$ in d) 153.14 mm e) 110 yds f) 432.5 yds
5 a) 320 cm² b) 204 mm² c) 88 ins² d) 4 cm² e) 3 ft² f) 8.52 m²
   g) 112 cm² h) 196 cm² i) 256.5 cm² j) 2 ft²
6 a) 32 cm² b) 7.7 m² c) 6.87 m² d) 3.218 m² e) 0.585 m²
7 a) 3 cm² b) 558 m² c) 247 mm² d) 102 ins² e) 112 cm² f) 7.2 cm²
8 a) 7546 cm² b) 314 ins² c) 78.5 m² d) 9.625 m² e) 30 184 mm²
9 a) 50″ b) 150.5 ins² c) 94 cm d) 502 cm² e) 911.5 mm² f) 5 129.5 mm²
   g) 401 m h) 395 m i) 398 m² j) 29.5 ft²

Volume and Capacity Practice

1 a) 24 cm³ b) 5 cm³ c) 0.45 m³ d) 0.852 m³ e) 0.125 m³ f) 32 ft³
2 a) 3.6 b) 75 c) 0.45 d) 5 263 e) 150 f) 5.6 g) $4\frac{1}{2}$ h) 58
3 a) 0.78 l, 175 cl, 2 400 ml b) 220 cl, 2 400 ml, 2.5 l c) 6.24 d) 259.2

Metric and Imperial Conversions Practice

1 a) 29 b) 2.5 c) 25 d) 29 e) 568 f) 1.1 g) 450 h) 3.3 i) 28 j) 2.2
2 a) 20 b) 11 c) 680 d) 0.88 e) 320 f) 264 g) 305 h) 2.3 i) 4.5 j) 91
3 a) £1.91/gal b) 39p/l c) 44p/l d) £1.80/gal e) £1.60/gal
4 a) 50 b) 68 c) 59 d) 39 e) 64 f) 10 g) 17 h) 28 i) ⁻7 j) ⁻13

Longer Problems (B)

1 a) £1.43 b) 5000 c) 0.751 d) 5.51 e) 6358 cm³
2 a) 279.4 b) 254 c) 228.6 d) 9″ e) 0.0672 mm f) 8.064 kg
3 a) $17\frac{1}{2}$ sq. ins b) 5.25 sq. ins c) 22.75 sq. ins d) 24 sq. ins e) 10p
4 a) 39.2° b) 40°F c) 13°F d) 27°F
5 a) £9.50 b) £6.30 c) £2.70 d) £10.35

Time and Timetables Practice

1 a) 3 hrs 15 mins b) 25 mins c) 2 hrs 20 min d) 1 hr 15 min
   e) 16 hrs 40 mins f) No. g) 4.05
2 a) 03.30, 20.30, 13.55, 10.47, 22.47 b) 3.45 am, 12.50 pm, 6.20 pm,
   9.37 pm, 12.05 am c) 11.50–14.05, 23.15–01.05
   d) 13.52, 12.10, 10.00, 00.07, 00.00 e) 5 hours
3 a) 10.32, 1 hr 35 mins b) 11.57 c) 20.57 d) 43 mins, 12.31, 48 mins
   e) 15.30, yes f) 35 mins

Speed Practice

1 a) 14 km/h b) 101 mph c) $4\frac{1}{2}$ ft/s d) 35.6 mph e) 12 km/h f) 80 mph
   g) 438 mph h) 424 mph
2 a) 11.18 am b) 2.48 pm c) 14.16 d) 3.30 am e) 00.57
3 a) 48, 64, 80, 96, 112 b) 31.25, 68.75, 81.25, 75, 56.25 c) 15, 14, 74

Average Practice

1 a) 3 b) 4 c) 3 d $5\frac{1}{4}$ e) 2 f) 7454.6 g) £151 h) 21.63 i) 163.3 m
2 a) 55 b) 1005 c) 6.5 d) 10 e) $2\frac{1}{2}$ f) 50

Ratio Practice

1 a) 2:3 b) 3:1 c) 3:2 d) 3:5 e) 1:6 f) 7:2 g) 5:2 h) 29.5:21 i) 4 j) £17.50
2 a) 1 km b) 250 m c) 10 m d) 4.5 km e) 5 m × 4 m f) 4.4 m × 2.5 m
   g) 80 cm × 1.65 m h) 13 m
3 a) 8, 4 b) £9, £12 c) 20 cm, 30 cm d) £42, £30 e) £320, £880

Gauges and Scales Practice

1 a) 175 ml b) 125 ml c) 290 ml
2 a) 40 lbs per sq. inch b) 28 lbs per sq. inch c) 77 lbs per sq. inch
   d) 51 lbs per sq. inch e) 6 lbs per sq. inch
3 a) 2000 rpm b) 3500 rpm c) 2750 rpm d) 4400 rpm e) 3300 rpm
4 a) 37.3°C b) 38.2°C c) 37.05°C
5 a) 2964 b) 7065 c) 807 d) 1247

Longer Problems (C)

1 a) 264 miles b) 44 mph c) 8 gals d) 0835
2 a) 54 ft b) 8 c) 5 yds × 4 yds d) 20 sq. yds e) $3\frac{1}{3}$ 1
3 a) 18 litres b) £9 c) 1.61
4 a) 42 g b) 284 ml c) 2:1 d) 32:3 e) 12.20
5 a) 40 mpg b) 9 gals c) 35.6 mpg d) 39
6 a) 50.4 m² b) 2597 c) 16
7 a) 43p b) 77p c) 14%
8 a) 4:3 b) 3.1 kg c) E10 d) 75p
9 a) 30% b) 2300 g c) 805 g
10 a) 7318 b) − c) 1327 d) £70.60
11 a) $\frac{1}{10}$ b) − c) 484 ml d) 198 mm
12 a) 48 mins b) 1445 c) 1610 d) 9 hrs 17 mins
13 a) 500 m b) 2 c) 5.75 km d) 1 hr 9 mins
14 a) £2.54 b) £3.81 c) £120.65 d) 2 hrs
15 a) £400 b) £63 c) £483 d) £84 e) £21